Proactive Risk Management

Proactive Risk Management

Preston G. Smith and
Guy M. Merritt

The material presented in this book must be appropriately tailored by a firm's management, based on its understanding of the firm's strategy, procedures, culture, and marketplace.

Most Productivity Press books are available at quantity discounts when purchased in bulk. For more information contact our Customer Service Department (800-394-6868). Address all other inquiries to:

Productivity Press
444 Park Avenue South, Suite 604
New York, NY 10016
United States of America
Telephone: 212-686-5900
Telefax: 212-686-5411
E-mail: info@productivityinc.com

Design and composition by William H. Brunson Typography Services
Proofreading by Mary A. Junewick
Printed and bound by Malloy Lithographing in the United States of America

Library of Congress Cataloging-in-Publication Data

Smith, Preston G., 1941-
    Proactive risk management : controlling uncertainty in product development / by Preston G. Smith and Guy M. Merritt.
        p. cm.
    Includes bibliographical references and index.
    ISBN 1-56327-265-2 (alk. paper)
    1. New products. 2. Risk management. 3. Product management.
    4. Uncertainty. I. Merritt, Guy M. II. Title.

HF5415.153 .S653 2002
    658.15'5—dc21

                                                        2002007100

06 05 04 03 02   5 4 3 2 1

CONTENTS

PREFACE

Witnessing teams develop new products, we have often been astonished to see "surprises" (that is, problems) pop up late in the project—which in fact should have come as no surprise at all. Indeed, in some cases, the very same problems had arisen before in other projects. In others, someone involved with the project suspected early on that a problem might occur, but no action was taken. (And such suspicions often remain entirely unspoken.) The developers fully intended to address a potential problem, but either a lack of time or a focus on other priorities prevented that from happening, and so that problem did not rise to a critical level of importance until it was too late.

Over the past decade, project management has become more sophisticated but no less amazing to observe. Most firms now use some variation of a stage gate product development process. Often built into this process is a step of identifying project risks and delivering a list of them at the initial gate. However, risk management usually ends with delivery of the list. Few development teams put much attention into managing risk, so they encounter needless surprises in schedule, product cost or features, project budget, team morale, or market acceptance. Even worse, the nature of these "surprises" is that they tend to come to a head late in the project, when it is difficult to do anything about them.

This regrettable situation need not exist. All pieces of the solution have been available in various places for some time. Yet, only in the last few years have a few companies assembled and integrated them into their development process in the way that they have done with, for example, stages and gates. Consequently, for most companies today, not only do surprises occur in a project, but similar surprises also tend to recur in project after project.

The prime purpose of this book is to enable product development teams to greatly enhance their management of project risks; that is, to identify these surprises early in the project and manage them throughout to diminish the disruption they cause. We lead you through a risk management process that has been used repeatedly and successfully at a few leading companies and suggest variations that you can make to adapt the process to your own needs.

On the surface, you may see nothing in our methodology that seems novel. Nothing critical in this book depends on advanced technology, recent research, or specialized software. However, there are some points crucial to success that we have seen in no other book. These include:

- a model of a specific risk that coalesces the team's energy around vital elements of a risk and its drivers, thus enabling the team to identify, prioritize, and manage major risks effectively;
- guidance on identifying drivers of risks, so that you can manage the root causes of a risk rather than its symptoms;
- appropriate quantification of the key factors of a risk, so that you can prioritize risks effectively without introducing errors that render your numbers meaningless;
- a clear distinction between a risk and an issue, which requires a different type of management;
- a host of supporting tools and strategies that will enhance any implementation of project risk management; and
- emphasis on the organizational and cultural impediments that can undermine implementation of an effective risk management program, as well as means of overcoming them.

In preparing this book, we reviewed much of the literature on project risk management. We made two observations:

- The risk management process covered here fits closely with the approach to managing risk suggested by the Project Management Institute (PMI®), the U.S. Department of Defense, and several project management and software development books.
- The depth of actual how-to information provided here on the risk management process does not seem to be available elsewhere.

Our conclusion: although the management process covered here is tailored to commercial product development and has been tested most thoroughly on product development projects, the process is applicable to many other types of projects with some adaptation. Furthermore, this book may provide more specific guidance than is available elsewhere for managing other types of projects.

Following good product development practice, we involved customers (potential purchasers of the book) in developing this product. An international customer council of 46 individuals made important contributions by suggesting additions or changes to the book's structure, completing 134 reviews of draft chapters among them, providing examples from their experience, and even selecting the book's title. Their countless suggestions have improved this book greatly. We are most grateful for all of the help and encouragement we received.

This material comes directly from the experience of project teams in applying this process and techniques. We have learned from them, for which we are thankful. We intend to keep expanding our knowledge of this vital field, so we are interested in hearing how this book works for you, what it lacks, and how you enhance these techniques. We look forward to hearing from you.

Preston G. Smith

New Product Dynamics

3493 NW Thurman Street

Portland, OR 97210 USA

Tel: +1 (503) 248-0900

Fax: +1 (503) 294-1192

preston@NewProductDynamics.com
www.NewProductDynamics.com

Guy M. Merritt

gmerritt60544@yahoo.com

INTRODUCTION

We have planned this to be a user-friendly, how-to book. Whenever possible, graphics illustrate concepts described in the text. The following icons in the margins draw your attention to important points in the text:

Icon	Name	Description
KEY IDEA	Key	Key points to remember
CAUTION	Caution	Pitfall; common mistake
EXAMPLE	Example	Specific application of the techniques
SCOPE	Supplementary Information	Insight helpful in broadening the techniques to other fields

Other Aids to Reading

We have deliberately kept this book concise, as our experience with management and project teams tells us that they have little time for reading and no patience for frills. However, if you find a point about which you would like to know more, check the annotated Supplementary Reading section at the end of each chapter, where we provide sources that are reasonably permanent and accessible. Also, we do provide abundant cross-references to other parts of the book, but we recommend that you use these only when you truly need more detail.

However, you do have to read at least part of the book! The pullout card at the back will be helpful only after you understand the process and the concepts it encapsulates.

KEY IDEA

In teaching this material, we have found that precise use of the terminology is crucial. If you ask 10 people to define *risk*, you will get 10 different definitions. Other critical terms can be more confusing. We provide two sources of help here. First, we have relabeled certain terms to render them unambiguous. For instance, we coin *expected loss* to avoid use of *risk exposure*, which some project risk management authors use, but it has several other meanings in the risk management literature. Second, there is a Glossary at the back of the book, which we encourage you to refer to (we kept it at our side while we were writing the book).

We quantify the severity of each project risk so that you can prioritize them and focus on those that are most severe. To do this, we recommend that all risks for a project employ the same units. When the units are monetary, this can be awkward, because *dollars* is ambiguous (there are Canadian, New Zealand, and Singaporean dollars, among others). Therefore, we arbitrarily pick one currency for each example to emphasize the need to be specific, as well as to provide an international perspective.

We present probabilities in two formats: 0.47 and 47 percent, for example, have exactly the same meaning.

The Book's Organization

Because *risk* has many interpretations, we suggest that you start by reading Chapter 1, which covers important points about project risk management and illustrates the types of risks that we will be covering. Without this grounding, you are likely to miss many critical points in other chapters.

KEY IDEA

Our foundation for identifying, analyzing, prioritizing, resolution-planning, and monitoring risks stems from a certain model of a risk. Chapter 2 describes this model and some alternatives. We suggest that you at least read the section there on the Standard Risk Model, because it ties together the critical elements of a risk that are the basis for the following chapters. This model is unlike anything we have seen elsewhere, so any expertise you may now have in project risk management is unlikely to substitute for comprehending this model.

The core of the book is a risk management process, covered in Chapters 4 through 8. Chapter 3 is an introduction to this process. It serves two purposes. Although not essential, it provides an overview of the whole process before you dive into it. Second, it serves as an executive summary—but only for executives; the project team will also need the details in Chapters 4 through 8.

The next five chapters cover the five steps of the risk management process:

- Chapter 4: Step 1—Identifying risks and their impacts (see the Glossary for definitions of these and following terms), preceded by the planning needed to initiate the process;
- Chapter 5: Step 2—Analyzing risks, including identifying their drivers, determining their likelihoods, and calculating their expected losses;
- Chapter 6: Step 3—Prioritizing risks, so that you can take action on the most important ones; a step that often appears only tacitly in other sources;
- Chapter 7: Step 4—Resolving risks, which includes alternative action planning approaches, such as transferring or preventing the risk and arranging a contingency plan should the risk event occur;
- Chapter 8: Step 5—Ongoing monitoring of action plans, retirement of successful plans, and identification of new risks that threaten the project.

Chapter 9 is a "toolkit" of analysis techniques useful daily in carrying out a risk management program, and Chapter 10 describes several risk management approaches that make you a more effective project risk manager.

KEY IDEA

Chapter 11, a critical one, offers advice on implementing a risk management program, integrating it into a product development process, and keeping it vital. If you wish to make these techniques "stick" in your organization, you must be sensitive to certain behavioral tendencies that we have experienced often in implementing these techniques—tendencies that few other management books mention explicitly. Consequently, if you have more than a casual interest in this subject, Chapter 11 is vital for management and quite useful for everyone else. In addition, the key and caution icons in the remainder of the book often relate to implementation issues.

Chapter 12 provides two case studies that guide you in applying project risk management to two specific areas: manufacturing ramp-up and embedded software development. They are intended to show how you can apply the risk management techniques described in this book to a variety of fields.

To recap, here is a short outline of the book:

- Chapter 1: Essential concepts of risk and risk management.
- Chapter 2: Risk models and the Standard Risk Model in particular.
- Chapter 3: An overview of the risk management process.
- Chapters 4 through 8: Details on the five steps of the process (see previous bulleted list for a breakdown).
- Chapter 9: Our risk manager's kit of analytical tools.
- Chapter 10: Approaches to effective risk management.
- Chapter 11: Implementation essentials.
- Chapter 12: Two case studies to illustrate how to use the techniques.

If you must minimize your reading, members of a project team should read Chapter 1, the first half of Chapter 2, and Chapters 4 through 8 at a minimum; management should read Chapters 1 and 3 for sure, and the "Standard Risk Model" section of Chapter 2 and Chapter 11, if possible.

Our style throughout is to present the principles and concepts first and then illustrate them with examples. For instance, Chapters 4 through 8 each have a case study at the end of the chapter that progresses throughout the five chapters. The last chapter, 12, offers two complete case studies that illustrate the technique suggested earlier throughout the book. If you learn more easily by seeing actual examples, please start with this material, and then return to the earlier material to broaden your appreciation of it.

Scope and Depth of Coverage

Product development is our field of expertise. We have also seen these methods used successfully in many projects outside of product development. For example, a reviewer of the whole book is an expert in construction management projects. However, we stay with product development throughout only to maintain continuity of presentation, and we try to use well-known products as examples to ease the burden on nonproduct developers.

If you intend to apply this material outside of product development, watch for three sources of help as you read the book:

SCOPE

- the manufacturing and software development case studies that are the subject of Chapter 12,
- the supplementary reading at the end of each chapter, and
- the supplementary information icons that provide alternative approaches that may fit your projects better.

Also, identify the special characteristics of your application—relative to product development—before you start the book. For example, if your interest is in service development, observe that services lack many of the manufacturing risks encountered in product development but have additional complications to keep in mind, such as being:

- less tangible,
- more variable from one customer to another, and
- more perishable (because services are often "developed" at the time they are sold).

By keeping these special characteristics in mind, you can adjust the techniques to another type of project.

Finally, keep in mind that you can apply the project risk management process and tools effectively to a single critical project. However, we encourage you instead to integrate these techniques into your development process (Chapter 11). In addition, train every product development team member in their use so that they are applied routinely to every project. In this way, they become part of an overall corporate learning process that leads to improved product development capability. Then project risk management will move beyond individual projects to address longstanding systemic weaknesses, such as an inadequate product development process.

KEY IDEA

We present this material from the perspective of practitioners who have completely implemented the techniques described and have seen them substantially improve business operations. When presented in this way to those just starting the journey, they can seem overwhelming or just "too much work." If you fit into this category, we urge you to read the book nevertheless, especially the section "How Much Risk Management?" in Chapter 1 and all of Chapter 11 on implementation. You will find many ways to scale down the full process and valuable techniques and perspectives to apply even if you do not implement the full five-step process. Chapter 11 will also guide you into a progressive means of implementing the full process and adapting it to your needs. Thus, we believe this book will be useful to beginners and advanced users alike.

1

WHAT IS RISK AND HOW IS IT MANAGED?

To open with a clean slate, we considered writing this book about "ksir"* rather than risk. Risk is a tainted term. Each of us has prior, often subconscious and unhelpful, associations with risk. Perhaps it recalls the life insurance salesperson who called during dinner last evening, or the high blood pressure reading the doctor took last year. Maybe it stems from a downturn in the economy and its implications for your job. If you are an engineer, risk may recall for you a design professor showing a film of the Tacoma Narrows Bridge collapse.

Narrowing our focus to *risk management* does not help much. An Internet search on "risk management" (in quotation marks) yields over a million hits, very few of which have any connection with this book's contents.

Consequently, let us substitute "surprises" for risks for a moment. This book is about managing surprises in a project environment. Rather than just letting surprises affect you, we will show you how to identify them beforehand, assess their consequences early on, and plan ways to render them harmless to the objectives of your project. Although we focus on projects to develop new products, the techniques apply equally well to other types of projects that you may encounter in industry.

If you are an engineer, you may think of a surprise in terms of a design of yours that fails in a field trial. If you are a marketer, the surprise may relate to that start-up competitor you assured your boss last month would be no problem. If you are an accountant, you probably envision surprises as being preceded by dollar, euro, or yen signs. You are all correct. To further clarify, we provide an example to illustrate the scope of project "surprise" management.

Example of Project Risks

To ensure that we have a common understanding of the types of project concerns that could be subject to risk management, we here provide an

---

*Risk spelled backward

EXAMPLE example to focus our attention on the scope of potential problems that risk management could address in a product development project. The product here is a household version of the postage meter found in offices. This machine would be a small appliance that could be charged with postal value through an encrypted telephone connection to a postage supplier under contract to the post office, and you would make payment to this supplier using your credit card. It would print the necessary postage either directly on an envelope or on special labels that could be attached to larger packages.

Below are some of the potential problems that could result in risks for such a project. It is not important that you comprehend the detail of each of these risks, but please observe the broad variety of uncertainties that could plague this relatively simple project. This list, as long as it is, is only a sampling. When we have shown the list to others, they can usually readily add even more risks. Nevertheless, this list suggests the scope of project risks that we address:

- Marketing
  - Will an Internet technology, such as Stamps.com™ (a supplier of U.S. postage over the Internet, which can be printed as stamps on your home computer), take over this market before we can exploit it?
  - Will market research show that the need for international and package rates is sufficient to add this complexity, or will domestic letter rates be adequate?
  - Would we miss a sizeable senior citizen market if we do not magnify the control panel and buttons and make the display print larger?

- Sourcing
  - Can the print head supplier meet our standards for indicating an out-of-ink condition?
  - Will we be able to get ample quantities of certain components that are on allocation?

- Regulatory
  - Will stricter governmental standards for auditing such devices, which are now under consideration, go into effect before we can launch our product?

- Will we find a cost-effective means of repairing these units without compromising the postal value that was in them when they failed?

- Technical
  - Although we do not now know all of the failure modes, can we design it to protect its postal value regardless of failure mode?
  - Can we meet corporate drop-test requirements with the relatively fragile display technology required to meet our cost targets?
  - Can we attain legible, indelible print quality on any type of envelope paper?

- Management
  - Will we obtain the sales force support needed to complete the specified field test?
  - Will the software specialists be available when needed to code the value transmission?

Observe two things about this list. First, it is specific to this project and market at this point in time. Second, it goes far beyond engineering items.

KEY IDEA

Risk Management and Product Development

Risk management is a fundamental component of project management. The Project Management Institute (PMI®) lists the management of risk in their Project Management Body of Knowledge (PMBOK®) as one of nine knowledge areas, along with the management of project scope, cost, and schedule. Project managers are thus trained to manage risk as an integral, ongoing part of a project, not just as an afterthought or when risks begin to disrupt progress.

Link this with the fact that we carry out product development as projects. Generally, each new product has a project associated with it. In some companies, the connection between projects and product development is implied, but in others, the leaders of projects are actually called project managers. Companies recruit individuals with project management skills and also train their own people in these skills so that development projects run more smoothly. It would be difficult to imagine a product development effort that did not have the project management tools of a schedule, a statement of scope, and a budget associated with it.

Given that risk management is an integral part of project management and that product development inevitably requires project management, it would seem that managing risk would occur as naturally as managing the schedule during a product development effort. This may be the case in a few years, but today genuine risk management often gets lost in the crunch to get the new product out the door.

KEY IDEA

The prime purpose of this book is to enable product development teams to greatly enhance their management of project risks—across the board. Some individuals are instinctively good at managing project risks, but others deny risk or are unaware of it until it happens. Our goal is to build project risk management methodology into the organization so that it does not depend on being an innate gift but is a way of life in the organization.

Risk is an essential characteristic of product innovation. Every decision regarding a project—whether made explicitly or implicitly—has risk associated with it. Going into a project, we know that we will have less than a complete understanding of the project's components, so we will have to take some risks and make decisions regarding these risks. That is, we are practicing risk management whether we prefer to or not.

Today's increased focus on time to market makes it a business imperative that a business assumes certain risks. At the same time, the importance of time to market intensifies the consequences of risks as schedule slippage becomes increasingly intolerable. In the past, it may have been acceptable to manage risk implicitly, but managing schedule risk explicitly is one area today that separates leading companies from ordinary ones.

Relative to other kinds of projects, product development carries additional elements of risk. Product development involves innovation, and an essential characteristic of innovation is that, regardless of where we start with it, there are always pieces of information that we need now that will not be known until we are further downstream. This leads to iteration or looping, and it means that we have to make some assumptions now based on incomplete information and then revisit our assumptions later to determine their validity. (For tools to deal with this iteration, see the section in Chapter 9 on "Design Structure Matrix.") Projects with considerable innovation have more of this guessing and looping than less innovative projects.

Consequently, no other type of project is in greater need of risk management than product development. At the same time, our experience tells us that few product development projects today receive adequate risk management. This is why—considering both the great need and the current weakness—this book centers on product development projects. The proven, cost-effective techniques provided here are your keys to enhanced product development risk management.

What Is a Risk?

In teaching this material, we have discovered that much of the confusion about managing risk stems from differing interpretations of many of the terms involved. This is understandable, because *risk* is a popular word in our daily vocabularies. However, this popularity can work against us in managing risk, where we have to be more precise in our thinking about it.

As applied to a project, a *risk* is the possibility that an undesired outcome—or the absence of a desired outcome—disrupts your project. *Risk management*, then, is the activity of identifying and controlling undesired project outcomes proactively.

KEY IDEA

For reference, as you work with these and other terms, we provide a glossary at the end of the book. However, we go to greater depth here to describe three essential facets of a risk: uncertainty, loss, and its time component.

UNCERTAINTY

As illustrated by our postage meter example, when you manage risk, you are always dealing with uncertainties. A risk may or may not happen, and you will not know for sure until the risk occurs, that is—until after it ceases to be a risk. This inherent uncertainty cannot be eliminated. However, you can often narrow the uncertainty by:

- clarifying the probability of occurrence of the risk,

- understanding the consequences or alternatives if the risk event happens, and
- determining what drives the risk, i.e., the factors that influence its magnitude or likelihood of occurrence.

Risk management helps you understand these factors as thoroughly as possible in advance and consistently sway them in your favor.

KEY IDEA

There is an important consequence of this inherent uncertainty: no matter how well you execute risk management, some risk events will still occur. *The uncertainty can never be completely eliminated*, only reduced to a degree that you find tolerable (later we cover choosing a tolerable level). In other words, risk management cannot guarantee that there will be no surprises!

CAUTION

As you will see in Chapter 4, when you are identifying project risks, some events that are certain to occur (or may have already occurred) will tend to creep in as risks. This is quite natural, and as you become more skillful in identifying risks, you will become sensitive to tagging as risks only those events that are *uncertain*.

Events that are certain to occur are known here as *issues*. They are just as important as risks, and you should capture them as they arise while identifying risks. However, they are managed quite differently, so, once they are identified, they proceed on a different action-planning track.

Because confusion between risks and issues occurs often when identifying risks, we provide an example. Consider the first risk listed for the postage meter example covered earlier, the risk of Stamps.com preempting the market. If Stamps.com had already taken over the market, then this event is a certainty, that is, an issue. You would have to decide now to find a new market, such as the non-U.S. market, or abort your project. On the other hand, if Stamps.com had not taken over the market yet, then you would have a risk with a certain possibility of happening. Your risk resolution plans could include accelerating development to beat Stamps.com to market or designing your machine to be more user-friendly or reliable than a computer to gain market advantage. Or, when Stamps.com's market penetration reached a certain level, you could abort your project then. The point is that your response would be quite different depending on whether Stamps.com's dominance is a possibility or a certainty.

LOSS

Recall the postage meter example: these risks can result in lost market share, lost production, higher warranty and repair costs, and similar losses. Risk always involves the possibility of a loss of some kind. We manage risk because we do not want to suffer the loss, even if it is only a remote possibility. If there is no loss possible, then we are not concerned about the risk, because it cannot compromise the project.

Notice that we say the possibility of a loss. When the risk occurs, there is a possibility that the outcome will be even better than if the risk had not occurred. For, example, perhaps your risk is the loss of a key manager. But when this manager actually leaves, it is conceivable that an even better manager could replace her, allowing your project to fare better than imagined before. This would be an unexpected benefit to the project. For some types of risk management, both loss and gain should be considered. However, our goal is the management of events that could have an adverse impact on the project, so we only look at the negative—and most likely—side of the situation. Thus, risk does always involve the possibility of a loss, which is the reason for managing it, even though the actual outcome could conceivably be a gain.

KEY IDEA

TIME COMPONENT

Associated with every project risk is a time when it no longer exists, that is, either you have suffered the loss or the risk has been resolved to the point that you are comfortable that it is unlikely to cause serious damage to the project. It is important to know when this time arrives, because you can then remove this risk from your agenda and quit devoting effort to it. Although there may be other time aspects of a risk, the important one is this termination time, because it plays heavily in how you manage the risk.

In some cases, the termination time could be distinct; in others, it is ongoing. For example, a risk might be that the next batch of prototype parts coming from a supplier might have cracks in them. Or, your risk could be that the cracks you have observed already in prototype parts could show up in production at any time. Note that the "time component" may not always be expressed as a time but manifest as a condition, a defect rate in this case.

If there is no time component, then the event is more of an ongoing nag—which is a general risk of being in business. For instance, you normally would not list a supplier's performance as a risk, but if you see in the news that the intended supplier has won a six-month contract from a large firm that could tax its capabilities, there may be a time component and thus a manageable risk.

Figure 1-1 illustrates how uncertainty, loss, and a time component can be used as criteria to ascertain that a risk candidate is genuinely one that can be managed.

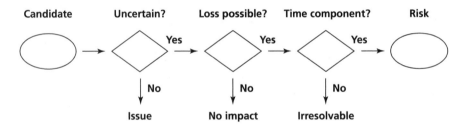

Figure 1-1. The three components of a risk, which determine our ability to manage it.

Why Companies Fail in Managing Risk

Although there may be other fundamentals of managing risk well, two—cross-functionality and proactiveness—stand out, because these are the two areas where we see companies fail to manage project risk repeatedly. If you do well at these, the rest of your risk management program will fall into place.

CROSS-FUNCTIONALITY

Too many companies—and their managers—fall into the trap of thinking that because most of the effort that goes into product innovation is technical, innovation can be relegated to the R&D department. This assumption is especially dangerous in the case of risk, inasmuch as most development project risks fall outside of R&D, even for high-technology products. Take another look at our postage meter example, which is fairly typical: only 3 of the 11 listed risks are technical ones.

Perhaps the best demonstration of preponderance of non-technical risk comes from Professor Robert Cooper. He has spent 25 years investigating the causes of success and failure in new products (see Supplementary Reading at the end of the chapter). His findings, based on research into nearly 2000 products in many industries and countries, are that success in product development depends primarily on (in order):

1. Unique, superior, and differentiated products.
2. Strong market orientation.
3. Sharp, early fact-based product definition.
4. Solid up-front homework (competitive, market, technical, and financial studies, for instance).
5. True cross-functional teams.
6. Leverage (building on core strengths).
7. Market attractiveness.
8. Quality launch processes.
9. Technical competence and technical activities executed well.

As you can see, only the last of these nine items resides solely in R&D. The others are either dominated by marketing or are cross-functional in nature.

If you presume that project risk resides primarily in R&D and turn risk management over to the technologists, you will simply miss many risks that will plague you later. According to Cooper's list, you will be addressing about one-ninth of the potential risk. Even issues that appear to be technical often cannot be resolved at a technical level. Take the cracked parts mentioned above, for instance. Resolving this risk may be a purchasing issue or even a legal issue, so addressing it on a technical level may not resolve it.

In this regard, you may be aware of failure mode and effects analysis (FMEA), a process that has similarities with ours. Engineers, especially in regulated industries, routinely analyze their designs using FMEA. Although

SCOPE

FMEA is valuable for what it does, it is aimed at a quite different objective than project risk management: ensuring that the *product* is designed and manufactured to be safe and reliable. In contrast, our objective is a successful *project*, so we will consider many objectives in addition to safety and reliability.

PROACTIVENESS

CAUTION

Typically, development teams make two timing mistakes regarding risk management. One is to wait until late in the project, when many risks start occurring, and then decide that they need to deal more seriously with risk. This creates three problems:

- Because the cost of making changes rises greatly during a project, late attention to risks often leads to expensive workarounds.
- Late discovery of potential problems precludes solutions that would have been available earlier.
- Late surprises are more disruptive to the schedule, due to our limited timeframe to develop adequate means of resolution.

The other timing mistake is to let risk management lapse. Because many firms now have risk-management deliverables built into early stages of their development process, the team does deliver a list of risks. Then they get on with the "real" work of developing the product. When the risk events start occurring, they are just as unprepared as the group who waited too long to even consider risks, but more embarrassed because they had been forewarned of the surprises.

Done well, risk management commences early in the project and proceeds as a monitoring and follow-up effort throughout, exactly as the team usually handles schedule management or cost management. Monitoring the risk list and progress being made on it can be a powerful way for management to really understand how a project is progressing, more powerful than the more common project control approaches of checking off deliverables as they are submitted or comparing actual against planned progress. It is more powerful because it is forward looking rather than looking at history.

The Antithesis of Risk Management: Firefighting

As you implement your project risk management program, it may be helpful to keep in mind the opposite of what you are trying to accomplish, an all-too-common type of management behavior often called "firefighting." Managers who excel in this behavior are not proactive—they are reactive. In fact, a "good" firefighter is so involved in fighting the last fire that he or she lets the next one smolder until it is almost hopeless. Then this person is regarded as a hero for pulling the new problem "out of the fire." It is a win-win situation for them: if they fail, they can't be blamed for not resolving such an irresolvable problem. Regrettably, this type of behavior is easy to reinforce. One observer of management noted that in any organization with at least three firefighters you would find at least one arsonist!

In contrast, good risk management is pretty dull. The risk manager obtains satisfaction and rewards for preventing fires from ever igniting. It is methodical, behind-the-scenes work, not a Hollywood action film.

It is easy to view firefighters as heroes and reward such behavior, thus reinforcing it. Consequently, firefighting is closely connected with corporate motivation and reward systems and with an organization's culture. Professor Robert Hayes, writing in the July–August 1981 issue of *Harvard Business Review*, observes that for American managers, "Crises are part of what makes work fun. To Japanese managers, however, a crisis is evidence of failure." What this means for you, in implementing a risk management program, is that you should be sensitive to and willing to confront reactive behavior and its motivators that threaten to undermine proactive risk management.

It is most unfortunate to professional firefighters that this behavior is so named, because they spend most of their time *preventing* fires—cleaning out areas where they might occur, and training and planning for them should they occur— not speeding around in blaring fire engines putting them out. Real firefighters are proactive.

Firefighting behavior is but one pitfall that can disable a risk management program. Others include the "kill the messenger" syndrome and bravado on the part of team members who believe they can handle any obstacle. We discuss these in Chapter 11.

How Much Risk Management?

KEY IDEA

Risk management can be overdone, as suggested earlier in the discussion of uncertainty. The reason is that effective risk management requires effort that otherwise could be applied directly to developing the product. The more risks you identify and the more thoroughly you analyze and monitor them, the more your risk management will cost.

Consider insurance. Some people buy insurance against automobile breakdowns, and others decide that they will self–insure against this risk, which after all is likely to have limited consequences. On the other hand, few of us could afford the consequences of a legal liability suit, so we insure against this risk.

Project risk management involves the same types of decisions. We *choose* the risks that we will manage, based on their consequences and likelihood and on the cost of resolving them. Some projects merit more risk management than others. On some projects (or portions of projects), you may *decide* to carry "high deductibles."

KEY IDEA

Two words were italicized in the last paragraph, because they are crucial. Good risk management requires that you make explicit choices and decisions, and that you revisit these choices and decisions repeatedly during the project. Do not let such choices and decisions happen by default. This is why risk management must be deeply embedded in your product development process. It is essential to developing products effectively.

On another level, some readers may find this book overwhelming. They are doing essentially no risk management now, and, in contrast, the process we suggest appears to be too much work. If this happens, you are probably considering the methodology too broadly. Projects vary considerably: small companies versus large ones, one-off products versus high-volume production, high-tech opposed to mature technologies, and major initiatives compared to facelifts. Consequently, your risk management process might include only a small part of what we cover. You must choose the portions that apply to your projects. We provide alternative approaches and suggest criteria for selecting.

Because of the variety of projects and organizations, no single process will fit all of them well. Any process that attempts to accommodate all projects, indeed, will be too much work for the smaller, simpler projects—which are likely to be the majority of your projects. You find what works for you only by experimenting. The material in Chapter 11 on continuous improvement and learning from your experience is crucial to selecting a level of project risk management that fits your business. Please keep track of what is working and not working effectively for you and adjust accordingly.

KEY IDEA

Project managers who do well at risk management spend substantial amounts of time doing it. This occurs because to them, project management *is* risk management. They have shifted into a mode of being proactive in managing their projects, and much of the time they spent formerly in fighting fires is now directed toward preventing risks. Thus, we think of project risk management not as more work but as a different style of work.

Risk As an Ally

Not only is it impossible to eliminate all risk and costly to overdo risk management, but it is also unwise to think only of eliminating risk. Sometimes, risk and uncertainty can lead to a net advantage—that is, an opportunity. If you drive out all risk as an evil, you will preclude opportunities that are the essence of innovation and product development. Innovative product development depends on exploring the uncertain to add product value and maintain competitive advantage.

CAUTION

Instead of routinely avoiding risk—being risk averse—consider each risk both in terms of what it can do for you and how it can harm your project. For instance, avoiding a new technology because of its risk will preclude your gaining from its potential cost–performance advantages. Explicitly consider the risks you undertake, and choose those whose upside outweighs their downside. As you get further into the book, we show you how to quantify your risks so that you can make these decisions wisely. If you would like a numerical illustration now, turn to "Consider Risk Also As an Opportunity" in Chapter 11.

Attitudes Toward Risk

Risk involves uncertainty, and uncertainty is measured by using probability. *Probability* is a curious concept, at the same time being something that is both intuitively comfortable and nonsensical. We appreciate that the weather forecaster tells us what our odds are for the day so that we can decide whether it is worthwhile lugging an umbrella around. This fits comfortably. But when this same forecaster says that the chance of rain is only 10 percent on our wedding day and it rains nevertheless, we feel tricked. It matters little that it failed to rain on nine other wedding parties under similar circumstances.

We use probability to analyze risks because it is the best tool we have. The theory of probability is built on controlled, fair experiments, such as a hundred rolls of a fair die. In project management—and especially in product development—you seldom have the opportunity to repeat the same activity frequently enough, or under adequately controlled conditions, for the theory to hold. Nevertheless, you proceed with the theory presuming that if you trust it, in the end it will, "on average," work to your advantage.

As we describe in detail in following chapters, we assess a risk by combining the probability of its occurrence with its consequence. Specifically, we multiply these two quantities. This too seems intuitive and comfortable, and it fits mathematical theory well. But controlled experiments by psychologists show that real people do not necessarily perceive risk in this way, nor do different people perceive the same risk to be equally serious. In particular, an individual can be risk averse, which means that person might avoid a risk even though the mathematics say that the risk is advantageous to take. In this book, we try to warn you of situations where your emotions may override more reasoned judgment.

Researchers have learned another interesting aspect of risk aversion: it is nonlinear. This means that you tend to operate according to the mathematics if the risk is relatively small. However, if the risk is large, you may tend not to take the risk; that is, you will be risk averse. This aspect of risk aversion is normal and healthy. We are more cautious with catastrophic, infrequent risks, for good reason. When we get into prioritizing risks in Chapter 6, you will see that we treat catastrophic risks in a special way.

We wish that we could present project risk management as a science or a fixed process, but this is not how it works. In the end, you will benefit greatly by discussing your risks—both within your project team and with management—to decide jointly what levels of risk you wish to accept and how risk averse the organization wishes to be.

Summary

Risk, unfortunately, has many meanings to people, so we have taken care to define it in terms of its three earmarks: uncertainty, loss, and a time component. We have also illustrated, through the postage meter example, the scope of project risks we address. Good project risk management places an emphasis on being both cross-functional and proactive. It is also the opposite of firefighting, which poses an implementation challenge for organizations in which firefighting is endemic. Finally, you cannot make risk management perfect; you *can* reach a point of diminishing returns; and it is unwise to consider risk only as being negative.

The next chapter covers the model of risk that is the heart of our methodology. If you have not already read the Introduction—immediately preceding this chapter—you will probably find it helpful in making the most of this book.

We close this and other chapters with some sources you can use to pursue topics in further depth. When looking for literature on risk management, keep in mind that this is a broad topic and that we are viewing it from the narrow perspective of projects. If you conduct a search on "risk management," you will find that the vast majority of the material applies to financial risks, either in the insurance industry or in such areas as mortgages or foreign currency transactions. Little of this information is useful to us. However, the next largest category is perhaps software risk management, and this is potentially useful. Much effort in recent years has gone into making software development a smoother activity, and hardware and service developers can learn much from the effort that has gone into managing software development.

Supplementary Reading

Cooper, Robert G. *Winning at New Products*. Third Edition. Cambridge, Massachusetts: Perseus Books, 2001. Cooper takes a holistic view of product development that makes it abundantly clear that risk management cannot be the exclusive domain of the engineer (see page 59).

A Guide to the Project Management Body of Knowledge. Newtown Square, Pennsylvania: Project Management Institute, 2000. Chapter 11 describes the nine knowledge areas of project management, including risk management.

Boehm, Barry W. *Software Risk Management*. Washington, DC: IEEE Computer Society Press, 1989. Broad coverage of software risk management that parallels the treatment in our current book well. Boehm has written four tutorials and supplemented each one with several more specific reprinted articles.

McDermott, Robin E., Mikulak, Raymond J. and Beauregard, Michael R. *The Basics of FMEA*. Portland, Oregon: Productivity, Inc. 1996. FMEA (Failure Mode and Effects Analysis) has many similarities to project risk management, which may provide some ideas for your risk management program. Its weakness is that it is not as proactive or as cross-functional as project risk management should be. This short (76 pages) book is a good primer on the subject.

2
USING PROJECT RISK MODELS

Our project risk management methodology—covered in Chapters 4 through 8—depends on a certain model of a risk that focuses attention on the critical attributes of the risk. Consequently, we start by introducing the model here. This model of a risk provides two important objectives. First, it helps you quantify the magnitude of a risk so that it can be compared against other risk candidates and help you decide which risks you are going to manage. Second, it points you toward root causes so that you can formulate effective plans to resolve your risks. Understanding the Standard Risk Model will help you understand the rest of the book.

As we were preparing this book, we spoke with many people about project risk. Each person had her or his special view of what constituted a risk and how that risk affected a project. Some who advocated a certain technique or philosophy, such as six sigma or quality function deployment, seemed to conceive of project risk in a way that happened to conform to that viewpoint.

Models give us a means to crystallize our viewpoints and make our concepts more tangible so that we can communicate them to others through graphics, mathematics, or words. This is extraordinarily helpful for a topic such as project risk, which is subject to various interpretations. Until a project team can reach understanding and agreement about the nature of the risks facing their project, they will not be able to take effective action against those risks.

KEY IDEA

Models are also valuable for reaching a common understanding about a risk situation. What are the basic inputs that influence the risk, how do they fit together in shaping the risk, and how does the risk's result manifest itself? What are the mechanics, the chain of events? Which factors are critical to the result, and which can be neglected safely? A good model, using an effective medium, will help resolve such questions.

Finally, models provide us with a systematic way of dealing with risk. They allow us to formulize a strategy to parse interactions and dependencies into components that we can manage effectively.

CAUTION

However, models also have weaknesses. They always represent only a partial picture of reality. No matter how complex we make them, there is always something missing. They often idealize relationships between their components. Consequently, you should have a healthy disrespect for models. They are helpful in gaining insight and agreement among the team, but if you let the models take the place of the reality they represent, you are apt to be blindsided.

Models may appear to be a rather theoretical, peripheral subject in a how-to book such as this. The "Supplementary Reading" for this chapter lists some highly regarded project risk management sources that do not mention models explicitly. We disagree, believing that models provide an invaluable aid in clarifying and unifying your team's thinking about a risk, thus helping you to formulate more cost-effective risk management plans.

In the following sections, we present some risk modeling alternatives. As you read about each of these models, consider it in light of the following criteria for judging the quality of a model:

- The purpose of the model should be clear; for instance, a risk model's purpose is to illuminate potential events that can adversely affect a project's success.

- The model should be user-friendly for its intended audience; as an example, a risk model should use terminology that is familiar to those assigned to the project.

- The model's framework should be universal to maximize reuse; as we will see with a risk model, one can use the basic format across many projects.

- The model's framework should allow independent users to develop similar results when using the same input data.

- The model's output should be verifiable by measuring the actual output of the modeled entity or by relying on previous behavior of existing entities, such as risks and associated losses that have occurred on past projects.

Standard Risk Model

We have found the Standard Risk Model to be the one most helpful in comprehending a project risk and its associated loss. Figure 2-1 outlines the Standard Risk Model.

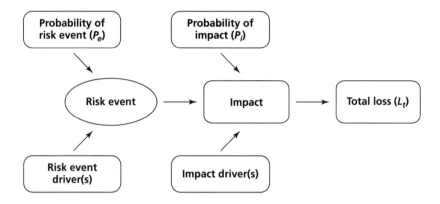

Figure 2-1. The Standard Risk Model is the preferred technique to model project risks.
Source: Adapted from Fastrak Training Inc. training material. Used with permission. ©1996.

The Standard Risk Model has several components:

- *Risk event:* The happening or state that "triggers" a loss.
- *Risk event driver:* Something existing in the project environment that leads one to believe that a particular risk event could occur.
- *Probability of risk event:* The likelihood that a risk event will occur.
- *Impact* (of a risk): The consequence or potential loss that might result if a risk event occurs.
- *Impact driver:* Something existing in the project environment that leads one to believe that a particular impact could occur.
- *Probability of impact:* The likelihood that an impact will occur, given that its risk event occurs.
- *Total loss:* The magnitude of the actual loss value accrued when a risk event occurs; it is measured in days or money (other quantities could used, but we recommend consistently using one unit, for instance, workdays *or* euros, throughout a project so you can compare risks easily).

This model has the strength of being fairly simple to understand. More importantly, it captures the essence of resolving risks. For instance, by referring to the left side of the model, notice that changing the risk event drivers can reduce the probability of the risk event occurring. Similarly, the impact portion (the three boxes in the center) helps you conceptualize ways to mitigate the total loss by changing the impact drivers, even if you cannot prevent the risk event from occurring.

Another important strength of this model is that it supports a cause and effect relationship. The risk event is the element that causes the impact and thus its total loss. One can also view the risk event as the cause of the impact. This reinforces the concept that effective risk management means being proactive regarding the prevention of risks. Remove the cause (the risk event) and the effect (the impact) will not occur.

CAUTION

Even though we prefer this particular model, it has weaknesses that need to be avoided. We have found that some inexperienced users of the model will try to formulate a risk event and impact that span a significant length of time. For example, someone may state the risk event as, "The project will not get fully staffed" and the impact may be, "The project's end date is in jeopardy."

While this risk is correct technically, the time from the risk event occurring to the impact could span several months, thus limiting your ability to effectively manage the risk. Consider a better formulation. First divide the risk into two components: risk event and impact. The risk event could be worded, "The manufacturing engineer, Austin Grant, will not be assigned by July 8." Now add fact-based risk event drivers such as, "Austin is currently scheduled for two weeks of training starting on July 8." The risk event drivers tell you why you believe the manufacturing engineer will be unavailable.

Now develop the impact, "Review of the new manufacturing production line, scheduled for July 8, will be delayed by four weeks." The impact drivers should tell you why the delay is four weeks (rather than the two weeks that the manufacturing engineer is in training). For instance, one of the impact drivers may be, "The contractor conducting the review will be leaving the country for three weeks starting July 15." The manufacturing engineer being unavailable *triggers* the loss of four weeks, but the impact driver determines the loss' magnitude.

The important point here is that the drivers of the Standard Risk Model are critical pieces of information you will use in risk resolution planning. To prevent the risk event from happening, you could simply defer Austin's training. If you cannot move the training (in other words, the risk event occurs), then you can determine if the contractor has an alternate person whom you could use for the review on July 22 (after the manufacturing engineer's training). Notice that you did not fully mitigate the loss since the review will still be two weeks late, but this is better than four weeks.

KEY IDEA

In addition to the Standard Risk Model, many other risk management models exist, and we have selected three of them to explore further:

- Simple Risk Model
- Cascade Risk Model
- Ishikawa Risk Model

In general, these other models either lack crucial features needed to manage risks well, or they demand considerably more effort to apply relative to any additional benefit they might offer. Consequently, we advise using the Standard Risk Model. If your reading time is limited, you can concur with this recommendation and move on to the next chapter now.

Simple Risk Model

The Simple Risk Model (Figure 2-2) combines the risk event and impact into a single entity along with the risk's probability of occurrence. The advantage in this approach is its simplicity, so users naturally gravitate to it. The Software Engineering Institute's Risk Taxonomy (see "Supplementary Reading" at the end of the chapter) is based on this model, although the model is not mentioned.

SCOPE

We have found that organizations not trained in risk management will usually develop risk statements that tacitly follow the Simple Risk Model. For instance, a project plan may identify the following risk: "We believe there is a 90 percent chance the required test equipment delivery will be

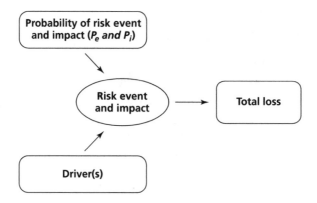

Figure 2-2. The Simple Risk Model has the luxury of being easy to understand but does not capture the full essence of risk management.

delayed by 30 days." Even though this is worded correctly, you cannot distinguish the risk event from its impact (the delay), so you are likely to have difficulty in finding effective ways of preventing the delay.

CAUTION

This model has the luxury of being simple to use, but this simplicity leads to confusion in being proactive about managing risks.

The simple model can expedite the risk identification and analysis processes, but it will ultimately cause confusion when you start risk resolution planning because you cannot distinguish drivers contributing to the risk event from those contributing to its impact. This is a critical distinction, because risk event drivers suggest proactive prevention plans. In contrast, impact drivers lead you down the reactive route to contingency plans so that you can take action on the impacts after they occur. Combining the risk event and the impact into one entity allows confusion to creep into the action planning process because you will be unable to distinguish readily between action plans designed to *prevent* the risks and those intended to *reduce* the losses should the risk events occur.

Cascade Risk Model

The Cascade Risk Model shown in Figure 2-3 is a multistage model with a risk event feeding a consequence driving an impact. In its simplest form it consists of three stages, but it could comprise many events cascading from one to another. To use an analogy, one can think of this model as a series of dominoes (three dominoes in the case of Figure 2-3) set up on their ends waiting for a push to knock them all down. Our experience has shown this model to be a good representation of how project risks unfold. In practice, rarely is an impact the direct result of a single risk event occurring. A loss that affects a project is likely to be a result of a series of cascading events that lead up to the loss. We have found this model to be useful when trying to understand the complex relationships that contributed to a catastrophic event or, more proactively, to further deconstruct a risk so that we can understand it better.

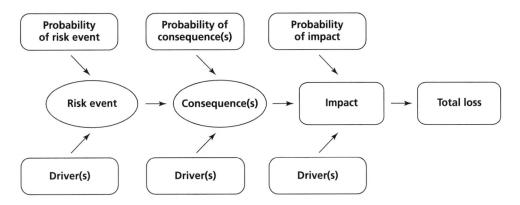

Figure 2-3. The Cascade Risk Model is a good approximation of how project risks unfold; however, calculating the probabilities can be difficult.

However, some organizations, in attempting to use this model for project risk identification, have developed so many cascading events that the probability of the risk occurring becomes remote.

For instance, assume one had a risk model with six stages with the following probabilities: 0.2, 0.6, 0.4, 0.8, 0.9, and 0.9. To determine if the risk will occur we simply multiply the probabilities together. The result of this calculation is only a 3.1 percent chance of occurrence for the specific risk. One concern readily becomes evident when using this model: the risk becomes so specific that it becomes improbable.

CAUTION

Another drawback of using this model for project risks is it requires a significant amount of effort to keep the probabilities accurate and up to date. Even though this model may be a better representation of project risks compared to the Standard Risk Model, you must strike a balance between model perfection and user-friendliness. We recommend using this model for a select few project risks that need additional deconstruction due to complexity, or in a retrospective analysis to learn why certain risks occurred and what their causes were.

Ishikawa Risk Model

Our last alternative is the Ishikawa Risk Model, or more suggestively, the "fishbone" model. This model is adapted from the quality management tool of the same name, which is designed to show cause and effect. Ishikawa models have the ability to depict many risk event drivers and risk events that cause a single impact to occur. Typical categories of risk events—such as people, process, product, and performance—are similar to those used with the quality management tool. Refer to Figure 2-4 for a graphical representation of this model.

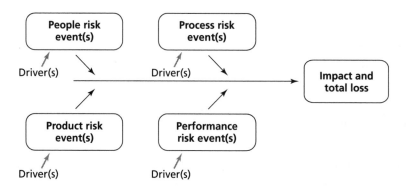

Figure 2-4. The Ishikawa Risk Model is the best representation of how a project risk occurs, but it is better suited to analyzing why the risk occurred in the first place than as a risk management tool. This example is based on the categories of people, process, product, and performance, but other categories can be used.

This model may provide the best representation of how actual project losses occur, but it also has the same problem as the Cascade model—many people find it overly complicated to use. In addition, performing probability calculations becomes extremely complex.

This model probably is better to use as a retrospective tool when analyzing why a risk occurred. As mentioned, real-world risks are likely to be the result of many risk events converging to cause an impact, which this model represents well. However, if you use this model as an action-planning tool, your team may become lost in the details. This model highlights the interactions and dependencies of categories (such as people, process, product, and performance) and how they influence projects, which is also helpful in retrospective analysis.

We cover retrospective analysis in Chapter 11. It is a valuable component of your risk management program because it can resolve recurring risks that project-by-project risk management would otherwise keep encountering. However, some companies make the mistake of doing only retrospective analysis and ignore project-specific risk management. This outlook is especially prevalent in firms that are heavily driven by a quality process. They tend to believe that if they perfect their process, it will isolate them from risk. Risk management will not prevent all risks from occurring, but project-specific risk management is your first line of defense against risks, many of which will differ from project to project.

Summary

This chapter described the benefits and downsides of models, along with a set of criteria to judge the quality of the models you employ. We described four risk models: Standard Risk Model, Simple Risk Model, Cascade Risk Model, and finally the Ishikawa Risk Model. We highlighted the strengths and weaknesses of these models, each of which can be used to assist project teams in proactively managing their risks. The Standard Risk Model provides the most effective risk management for the effort expended in using it. To further help compare and contrast the different risk models, refer to Table 2-1.

As you have learned, risk models provide a powerful tool to help visualize and understand risk. However, consider a word of caution from George Box, the noted statistician: "All models are wrong. Some models are useful."

Table 2-1. Pros and cons of different risk models

Risk Model	Pros	Cons
Standard	• Model framework is easy to understand • Separate risk event reinforces the notion of prevention (being proactive) • Separate risk event and impact supports cause and effect concept	• Model allows a significant time span to lapse between the risk event and the impact • Model does not allow multiple risk events to converge on a single impact
Simple	• Model framework is easy to understand	• The risk event and impact are combined into a single entity, which obscures the notion of prevention • Model be can confusing when developing prevention and contingency due to risk event and impact being combined • Model does not allow multiple risk events to converge on a single impact
Cascade	• Very good representation of how risks occur on projects • Separate risk event reinforces the notion of prevention • Separate risk event and impact supports cause and effect concept	• Model framework can be complex • Probability calculations can be complex
Ishikawa	• Best representation of how risks occur on projects • Separate risk event reinforces the notion on prevention • Separate risk event and impact supports cause and effect concept	• Model framework can be very complex • Probability calculations can be very complex • Because risk events are divided into categories that may interact, it can be difficult to state a risk event cleanly

Supplementary Reading

A Guide to the Project Management Body of Knowledge. Newtown Square, Pennsylvania: Project Management Institute, 2000 (pages 131–132). This guide, which covers project management generally, tacitly suggests an Ishikawa Risk Model with the following four categories: technical, quality, or performance; project management; organizational; and external.

Taxonomy-Based Risk Identification. CMU/SEI-93-TR-6, Pittsburgh, Pennsylvania: Carnegie Mellon University, 1993. This 90-page technical report outlines a specific technique for risk identification. This technique yields risks that fit with the Simple Risk Model. Although it is intended for software development, the questionnaire in this report is an excellent source for probing into potential problem areas in many types of projects.

Wideman, R. Max (editor). *Project & Program Risk Management: A Guide To Managing Project Risks & Opportunities*. Newtown Square, Pennsylvania: Project Management Institute, 1992, pages III–6. A description of risk in terms of the Simple Risk Model.

3

THE RISK MANAGEMENT PROCESS

Chapters 4 through 8 describe a five-step process for managing project risk, each chapter covering a step. These chapters present detailed material and suggest many variations to consider in adapting it to your needs. However, to aid in keeping the complete picture in perspective as you proceed, we'll begin with an overview of the five steps. This overview also serves as an executive summary for those who would like to understand the process without delving into its details.

The process described here is the one used by major telecommunication equipment and defense communication equipment manufacturers, and for continuity it will form a unifying theme throughout the next five chapters. This version has successfully mitigated losses in many projects—indeed, many of its specific elements were discovered through experience in applying the process to actual projects. In subsequent chapters, we highlight these discoveries to make you aware of potential missteps that lurk as you adapt the process to suit your business and its environment.

Overview of the Process

Figure 3-1 shows the flow through the five-step process and lists deliverables from each step:

- Step 1 – Identify risks that you could encounter across all facets of the project.
- Step 2 – Analyze these risks to determine what is driving them, how great their impact might be, and how likely they are.
- Step 3 – Prioritize and map the risks so that you can choose those most important to resolve.
- Step 4 – Plan how you will take action against the risks on this short list.

- Step 5 – On a regular basis, monitor progress on your action plans, terminate action plans for risks that have been adequately resolved, and look for new risks.

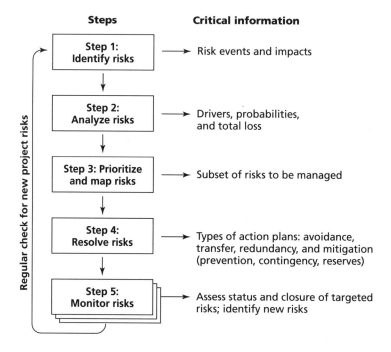

Figure 3-1. The five-step risk management process and critical information from each step. The first four steps are usually done once, but the last one is ongoing.

SCOPE

These steps are fundamental to managing risk, so even when you modify the process—perhaps streamlining it, adding more detail to it, or changing the nomenclature—you will still undertake these five activities. Recognizing these basic steps will help you to adapt the process to other applications.

Also, keep these five steps in mind if you consult other sources in refining your process. You can expect to see these steps there too, and this will help you to correlate other approaches that may differ somewhat. In particular, you are likely to see two apparent differences when comparing the process shown in Figure 3-1 with others. One is that most risk management processes start with a planning step. We cover these planning activities at the beginning of our Step 1 (identifying risks) because we believe that risk management planning should be integrated into project planning as much as possible, not treated as something special—and thus optional. The other difference is that we explicitly include a risk prioritization step, as we believe that this step is critical to success. Many others tend to combine prioritization with the preceding or following step, often simply implying prioritization.

Step 1: Identifying Project Risks

Because this step launches the process, you need to do some planning and preparation before you begin. For example, you will need a facilitator, preferably one without a stake in the outcome; an amply supplied meeting room; a solid definition of the project, specifically including any unusual features; and a schedule, development process chart, prompt list, or other means of eliciting specific project risks.

In this initial step, you identify risk events and their consequences that could prevent the project from meeting its defined goals of scope, schedule, cost, resource consumption, or quality. This is truly a discovery or brainstorming activity. Although it is best to keep in mind that a manageable risk involves uncertainty, the possibility of loss, and a time element, this should be a freewheeling activity rather than one that judges contributions at this time. Chapter 4 suggests various techniques you can use to uncover risks; primary among them is posting a large copy of the project schedule on the wall and having the whole team place stickies in areas of the schedule where they see risks. To get a broad view of the project, be sure to involve a cross-functional team.

Risk identification should be performed as part of a project's initial definition process, along with project planning, budgeting, and scheduling. In fact, these other activities cannot be done realistically without taking risk into account. In some cases, the risks discovered could cause the project to be abandoned or modified greatly during the planning stage. Also, explicitly scan for new risks throughout the project at team meetings, project updates, and at major milestones and phase completions.

KEY IDEA

A risk event should precisely describe a happening that *could* occur, along with an associated time component or condition so that one can tell if the risk event has occurred. For instance, a team member could state the following risk: "Engineering may not have enough resources to complete the project on time." The problem with this statement is that one cannot tell whether the risk occurred until the project has been completed. A better statement would be: "A graphical user interface [GUI] software engineer will not be available to review the system requirements until 15 days past the scheduled review on August 7." Now no one will misunderstand which engineering resource you are concerned about and when the risk could occur.

Each risk event should also be accompanied by its impact; that is, the loss that the risk event could cause. Using the previous example, an impact could be stated as, "Since our contract with our customer contains a penalty clause for missed program milestones, a 15-day slip in reviewing the system requirements will result in a ¥750,000 penalty." The ¥750,000 would represent the total loss.

The objective of this risk identification step is to get any identifiable risks on the table for discussion. Remember, this is a brainstorming activity, so even if you are skilled in limiting your risks to those that conform to the requirements of uncertainty, potential for loss, and a time element, you are likely to identify far more risks than you can pursue. The theme of brainstorming is that quality lies in quantity, so you strive for quantity first, and then sift through the results looking for the risks most likely to threaten your project.

Step 2: Analyzing Risks

In this step, you begin a selection process by being more specific about the magnitude of each risk candidate. We suggest that you analyze your project's risks by using the Standard Risk Model, shown in Figure 2-1.

The purpose of this phase of the risk management process is to develop drivers for each risk event and its impact. Drivers are existing facts in the project environment that lead one to believe that a particular risk event or impact could occur. For instance, why do we believe the GUI software engineer will be 15 days late to review the system requirements? Because we have discovered that this same engineer is also scheduled to perform field upgrades during the review period. One of the most important attributes of a driver is that it does not have a probability associated with it. Drivers need to be as close to being factual as possible. However, an exception does exist. Historical data should be so compelling that you could call it fact, such as: "In our previous 12 projects, GUI software engineers have not been available for 10 of the 12 system requirements reviews."

KEY IDEA

As shown in Figure 2-1, other vital pieces of required data for risk analysis are the two probabilities, one for the risk event and another for its impact. These probabilities are subjective and should be derived from the risk and impact drivers developed earlier. Historical project data may provide good estimates of probabilities rather than relying solely on subjective estimates.

Our experience has shown that the organization should decide on a small set of values to be used for stating probabilities. For example, one company allows only the values of 10, 30, 50, 70, and 90 percent. If you do not establish such rules at the outset with your project teams, you will find yourselves arguing needlessly over whether a probability is 23 or 27 percent. Risk events will never have a probability of 100 percent since it then would not be a risk but rather an issue that the team must address. However, impacts can have probabilities of 100 percent, such as in our GUI design example where a contractual penalty is being used for late delivery at project milestones.

CAUTION

All of these factors enter into calculating expected loss, as shown in Figure 3-2. Should you be concerned about this equation, rest assured that you are not likely to need mathematics any more complex than this to manage project risks. The challenge in project risk management is

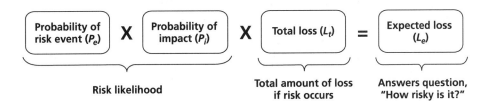

Figure 3-2. Formula for calculating expected loss from its components.

more in obtaining fact-based input values than it is in manipulating them mathematically.

Expected loss is the average (mean) loss associated with a risk. For example, for the GUI software engineer, say that you have estimated that there is a 30 percent chance that this engineer will actually be involved in field upgrades when also needed for your project. Consequently, P_e = 30 percent. Because P_i = 100 percent and L_t = ¥750,000 for this example, the expected loss for the GUI engineer risk is ¥225,000. This means that, on average, over a large number of projects, this problem is going to cost the project ¥225,000. If the GUI engineer actually is unavailable, the loss will be the full ¥750,000, but this is scaled down, on average, because it is only likely to happen 30 percent of the time. If you are quantifying losses in monetary terms, then expected loss is identical to what is often called expected monetary value (EMV).

KEY IDEA

Of all of the quantities we have just introduced, expected loss is central because it is your primary means of comparing and prioritizing various identified risks as you move into the next step. It is the main criterion you will use to decide to actively manage some risks and defer action on others. Unfortunately, it is also the quantity that has the greatest variety of names associated with it. Some others in the project management community call it *risk exposure*. We avoid risk exposure since the term has a different meaning in nonproject environments such as medicine, finance, and insurance. We believe that *expected loss* sidesteps the confusion surrounding risk exposure and also conveys the meaning of this quantity more clearly.

Step 3: Prioritizing and Mapping Risks

The purpose of this phase of the risk management process is to cull from your long list of risks a short list that will be managed actively. Expected loss is the prime criterion for conducting this culling, because it measures the damage that you can expect to be inflicted on the project by each risk. Other criteria, such as urgency, the cost of mitigation, or the catastrophic nature of a risk, may influence this short list. So that you can compare your risks, express all expected losses on the same scale, usually either days of delay or a specific financial unit.

You must prioritize because you have only limited resources to work on all the risks you can identify. To minimize and focus your effort, you will manage only the ones that make the short list. You might decide to add a catastrophic risk to the list, even though its probability is quite low. The point is to manage the risks that could cause the greatest damage to your project.

This is an important point. It may be unsettling to know that there are quite real and significant project risks that have been identified but will not be resolved. On the other hand, as you will see in the next step, each risk on the managed list will need significant resources, so you simply have to draw the line somewhere. There are really only two questions to consider: on what basis you draw the line, and how far down you draw it.

KEY IDEA

Notice that this relates to a couple of points made in Chapter 1. First, it is not possible to completely eliminate risk from a project and, second, you do reach a point of diminishing returns in pursuing risks of which you are quite aware. By prioritizing your risks, you apply your resources most cost-effectively according to the requirements of your project.

We mention here a simple technique used routinely at Tellabs, a telecommunications and broadband equipment manufacturer. Tellabs simply builds a "top 10 list" of the risks they will manage actively. There is nothing magical about the number 10. Indeed, often this top 10 list has more or fewer than 10 risks on it. Ten is just a convenient number of about the right size that Tellabs has found to be an effective balance between managing too few risks and managing too many. The beauty is in the simplicity here: due to their risk management training, everybody at Tellabs knows just what the top 10 list means and what to do with it.

Regardless of how you decide on the risks you will manage, you should also develop a risk map, as shown in Figure 3-3. This map displays two important quantities for each risk: total loss on the x-axis and the risk likelihood ($P_e \times P_i$, see Figure 3-2) on the y-axis. This map helps you balance your prioritization. If you simply use expected loss you might miss a catastrophic risk that has a total loss with a very high value but a low likelihood. For example, if a risk has an expected loss of four days, it may not reach the list, but if the total loss is a 45-day slip in the schedule, the team may decide that this risk is so catastrophic that they must put it on the list. The risk map provides an excellent display of the risks you have identified, so it can

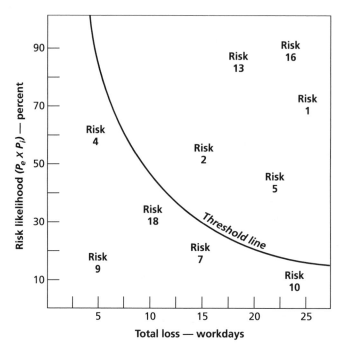

Figure 3-3. A risk map showing risks 1, 2, 5, 13, and 16 under active management and five more monitored candidates.

greatly assist in seeing which high-loss risks need to be included on the list. It will also be useful for the team and management to use on an ongoing basis to monitor risk, as your risks will migrate on the chart over time.

A threshold line, drawn at a constant level of expected loss, separates the risks under active management from those that are candidates for being managed later. Like the concept of expected loss, risk maps are often used in other areas of risk management. For instance, they are helpful in the insurance industry, where they are used to separate catastrophic risks from lower-impact ones. Sometimes they are called risk charts or risk diagrams in other applications, and they may have their two axes interchanged.

SCOPE

Step 4: Planning Resolution of Targeted Risks

The purpose of this step of the risk management process is to develop an action plan for each risk that you have decided to manage. Recall from the discussion at the beginning of Chapter 1 that many companies complete the risk management steps up to this point, and they even deliver a list of project risks at a phase review. However, they typically fail in resolving the risks because the project is now usually at a point where its intensity increases, and this diverts attention from risk management. The team must use constant vigilance to prevent the solid risk management work already completed from being set aside before it yields benefit.

Each risk that will be pursued receives an actionable plan for resolving it. Figure 3-4 shows the essentials of such plans. Following good project management practice, these plans include the same elements as any other project task, such as laying out a printed circuit board or testing a prototype. However, because risk resolution tasks are often small ones, you can use streamlined techniques to manage them, as long as you ensure that you provide the essentials in Figure 3-4.

An action plan has:

- An objective
- Means of measuring when the objective has been achieved
- A completion date
- A responsible individual
- Adequate resources allocated to complete the task

Figure 3-4. An action plan becomes an actual task in managing the project, and as such, it follows these same good management practices as any other task in the project.

The first two items in Figure 3-4 are particularly important because, unlike a more tangible task (such as the printed circuit board), it is not so clear when the risk management task is completed. The task is completed either when the risk actually occurs or when its expected loss is managed down to a level where it falls below the threshold line on your risk map. Because this task is consuming resources, you will want to terminate it as soon as you can, and having a task objective and a completion criterion clarifies this termination point.

KEY IDEA

CAUTION

However, the last three items in Figure 3-4 are also important, because without due dates, responsible individuals, and resources, action on resolving the risk is just a dream. By building such action plans into your project plans, just as you would for hardware development tasks, you establish risk management as a legitimate part of the project, and—more broadly—you institutionalize risk management as a normal expectation of product development.

As described in greater detail in Chapter 7, your action plans are of four types: transfer, redundancy, avoidance, and mitigation. Transfer and redundancy act upon the risk event itself, whereas avoidance and mitigation action plans will focus on the risk drivers (i.e., those facts leading you to believe why a certain risk will occur).

KEY IDEA

Action plans based on mitigation can be further refined into prevention plans, contingency plans, and reserves. Prevention plans are designed to deter the risk event from ever happening. The key to preventing risks is not to focus on the risks but to change their risk event drivers. Let us illustrate. In our example risk, recall that the GUI software engineer might not be available for a review, and the risk event driver was that this engineer was already scheduled to perform upgrades in the field. In this example, a simple prevention plan may be to look for another software engineer to perform the field upgrades.

Remember, not even the best prevention plan will keep all risks from occurring! This is why you also need contingency plans or reserves for your risks. Continuing with our example, assume that the GUI engineer was not available to review the system requirements. You could have had a contingency plan developed in advance to allow the review to proceed without the GUI engineer. In some cases, even a contingency plan does not mitigate the risk acceptably, and then you will have to establish reserves of time, money, or other resources, according to the type of loss that could occur.

In short, prevention plans work to deter the risk event; contingency plans and reserves work to minimize the loss if the risk event does occur.

Step 5: Monitoring Project Risks

This last step of the risk management process is explained in Chapter 8. In monitoring risks, you regularly review progress on your action plans—

transfer, redundancy, avoidance, and mitigation—to ensure that they make the desired progress and remain effective.

In addition, regularly look for changes in the external environment that may affect your action plans. For instance, the company may delay plans for the field upgrade, so that either this driver of the GUI software engineer's availability disappears totally, or the probability of the risk event occurring diminishes greatly. This may allow you to terminate this action plan. On the other hand, the environment in which your project operates changes continually, potentially exposing new risks that you have not noticed before. Consequently, you should execute a condensed version of the risk identification step on a regular basis. Unless you build this re-identification into your regular risk management reviews, it is likely to be neglected.

You can use several types of metrics to monitor progress on your risk management plans. For example:

- monitoring expected losses for your managed risks (if the action plans are working, expected losses should be declining);
- reviewing the number of risks successfully being prevented, which provides a reliable method of determining prevention plan effectiveness;
- reviewing the number of impacts successfully being mitigated when risk events do occur, which indicates the health of your contingency plans; and
- noting new risks appearing in your analyses, which indicates that you are remaining in touch with changes in your environment.

Risk management activity must be the center of attention at project meetings. The project manager should review progress on the managed list at each meeting, and the group should explicitly decide on additions to or removals from this list. Use a short brainstorming activity to identify any new risks. Project meetings, assuming they occur weekly, are your primary battle-lines against project risks, because management or phase reviews seldom occur frequently enough to provide effective risk management.

In addition, risk management status should be reviewed with management on a regular basis. The risk map is a particularly good way of portraying the current risk management situation to management. In fact, a thorough review of project risk is a particularly effective way for management to determine the health of a project, compared with the more common method of checking deliverables and completion of planned activities, for two reasons. First, completion of planned activities and deliverables is basically backward looking, whereas monitoring risk status provides a forecast of the hurdles that lie ahead. Second, reviewing the risk picture fits well with the management approach of managing by exception, the outstanding risks being the looming "exceptions." If a project's risk is being managed well, there are unlikely to be many surprises at the next review.

Summary

This chapter has been an overview of the five-step risk management process. In general, it starts in a structured brainstorming mode to list any possible risks that may jeopardize the project. Then, you analyze each risk you have found according to a regimen that will clarify the risk's relative threat to the project. From the most threatening risks, you choose a set that you will manage actively and create action plans for managing them. The last step then shifts to ongoing surveillance of your risk picture to ensure that managed risks are being resolved and any new ones come under management.

At this point, you can proceed into the next five chapters to study the details of the five steps, respectively, or you can skip to the chapters in the back of the book to learn about other aspects of project risk management.

Supplementary Reading

A Guide to the Project Management Body of Knowledge. Newtown Square, Pennsylvania: Project Management Institute, 2000. Chapter 11 is a 20-page treatment of the project risk management process that fits well with our Chapter 3 and further illuminates it. This body-of-knowledge material also illustrates how the steps of the risk management process described here dovetail with accepted good practice.

Conrow, Edmund H. Risk management. Chapter 17 in Kerzner, Harold, *Project Management*, Seventh Edition. New York: John Wiley, 2001.

Outlines a project risk management process encouraged by the U.S. Department of Defense to meet its system acquisition requirements. This DoD process, developed for very large projects, aligns closely with the one we have outlined in our book.

Martin, John E. and Heuime, Pierre-François. Risk management: Techniques for managing project risk. Chapter 12 in Cleland, David I. (editor). *Field Guide to Project Management*. New York: John Wiley, 1998. An alternative overview of the risk management process by a consultant and a trainer at IBM.

Portny, Stanley E. *Project Management for Dummies*. New York: Hungry Minds, Inc. 2001. Chapter 14 is a light-hearted but effective treatment of the project risk management process with many good tips.

Smith, Preston G. Managing risk as product development schedules shrink. *Research-Technology Management* 42(5):25–32 (September–October 1999). Includes an overview of the risk management process with many industry examples illustrating how product developers apply the principles.

4
STEP 1—IDENTIFYING PROJECT RISKS

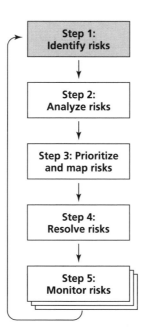

Each of the next five chapters covers one step of the five-step risk management process. If you have not already done so, we suggest that you first read Chapter 3, which provides an overview of the five steps. This will allow you to absorb these chapters more efficiently.

We cover risk identification here as though it occurs once, at the beginning of the project. In reality, a miniversion recurs regularly throughout the project to catch new risks, as described in Chapter 8.

Plan and Prepare

Some project management sources suggest starting with a separate risk-management planning step, which would include meetings, methodology, roles and responsibilities, budgeting, and scheduling, specifically for the risk management portion of the project. We believe that this segregated risk management planning perpetuates the nonintegration of risk management into the rest of the project. Risk management should naturally be included in the budgeting, scheduling, and other planning activities for the project as a whole. Thus, our emphasis is more on preparing for the risk management activity rather than planning for it.

An exception occurs when working on projects that involve several engineering groups, such as a project with multiple development contractors. In this environment, it is common for the project not to use a common product development process. Therefore, you should explicitly define and plan how risk management will be implemented regarding meetings, methodology, roles, and responsibilities.

You will essentially be running a brainstorming session, so prepare accordingly. Get a quiet room with plenty of wall space. Have on hand plenty of paper to line the walls, along with markers and sticky notes.

KEY IDEA

Obtain a skilled facilitator who does not have a significant part in the actual development. Much of your success in risk identification depends on appointing a skilled, independent facilitator. If your project manager qualifies, fine, but if this person is also vested in large parts of the development work, he or she will be compromised in trying to both facilitate the session and identify risks. In addition, if the facilitator is a contributor to the development effort, biases may creep into the risk list due to assumptions and perceptions the facilitator may have acquired in organizing the project. In other words, do not expect the facilitator to contribute any risks to the list.

Since risk identification—to be proactive—is best initiated early in the project, you may have access to only limited material about the nature of the project, but some definition of the project is essential to being specific about its risks. You should have on hand the business case; product requirements or specifications; any specific plans relating to the project, such as budgets, markets served, or supply chain partners involved; and an integrated (cross-functional) schedule.

Prepare a spreadsheet or similar template that you can use for logging and tracking risks as you move through the five steps. The tracking spreadsheet will become an essential element of your risk management process because it will contain the relevant risk data and resolutions. In Chapter 8 we present an example of an entire risk-tracking spreadsheet. You will ultimately be entering the following items for each risk (these items will be explained as they are encountered later in the process):

- risk identifier (for example, R1, R2, R3)
- risk owner
- risk event
- risk event driver(s)
- probability of risk event
- impact
- impact driver(s)
- probability of impact
- total loss
- risk likelihood
- expected loss
- priority

ASSEMBLE A DIVERSITY OF OPINION

As noted in Chapter 1, project risk is very much a cross-functional phenomenon. Because the majority of the people on your project are likely to be engineers, it is natural to huddle a group of engineers and do a wonderful job of identifying technical risks. But data in Chapter 1 demonstrate that only a minority of project risks are technical in nature. Thus, without true cross-functional involvement, you will inevitably miss most of the project's risks.

CAUTION

At a minimum, include the functions involved in developing the product: product engineering, software development, and manufacturing engineering. To guard against only identifying technical risks, consider adding the following functions: sales, marketing, sourcing, production, quality, and finance. The exact representation will vary depending on the nature of the project. (In one case we invited a corporate lawyer because we were concerned about significant product liability issues.) Rank in the organization should have no effect on an individual's contribution, but beware if it does.

If you developed a similar product recently with another team, you might include a member of that team. More broadly, you might consider someone from inside or outside of the company with broad industry experience.

VERIFY RISK MANAGEMENT KNOWLEDGE AND EXPLAIN PROJECT DETAILS

When you gather your diverse crew, however, you will have to prepare them so that their ideas are truly relevant. In addition to a general understanding of your product development process, they need two types of preparation—in the risk management process and in the project under consideration.

As for the risk management process, each participant must understand the material in the first two chapters of this book, especially the definition of risk and the factors and quantities entering the Standard Risk Model. If participants are not trained in the risk management process, they will identify issues rather than risks (see Chapter 1 or the Glossary for the distinction) and argue endlessly over the terminology.

Regarding the project, all participants should receive a briefing on the significant features and the novelties of both the project and the product. We have found it imperative to bring each participant up to a solid level of project understanding *before* the brainstorming session. Your briefing should answer the following questions, which we call the Product 5Ws:

- What is the project scope in terms of product features and functions?
- Who is the customer for the product, and how might the customer use or abuse it?
- Why does the company want to develop this product now (strategy, financial expectations)?
- Where is the product going to be deployed or sold?
- When does the customer need it?

In addition to the Product 5Ws, your team must understand the Process 5Ws—relating to the process of developing this product, as distinct from the risk management process mentioned above. Provide answers to these questions:

- What will your team develop internally, and what will external partners provide?
- Who will be developing each development portion?
- Where will the product be developed, integrated, tested, and manufactured?
- When do you believe you will be able to deliver the product?
- Why were those decisions made on the above four Process Ws?

Project scope and schedule—and their drivers—are particularly important, as are any unusual business partners (such as a contract developer or overseas manufacturing) or variations in your business model (for example, if this is the first time you will be selling the product online as well as through traditional channels).

By gaining clear insight into the Product and Process 5Ws, the product development team will sharpen their understanding of the risks being identified, thus enabling them to develop effective risk resolution strategies. For example, understanding exactly where certain subassemblies are developed and manufactured can shift risk into or out of the project.

GET PARTICIPANTS THINKING CREATIVELY

To get people thinking "out of the box," you might warm up with an exercise to stimulate their creativity, such as listing 50 ways that they could use some strange contraption you place before them if they were stranded on a desert island. Precede this by reviewing guidelines for brainstorming:

- Provide a clear initial problem statement.
- Do not judge contributions!
- Encourage cross-fertilization, piggybacking, and further development.
- Draw out off-the-wall ideas.
- Emphasize quantity (quantity breeds quality).

For more ideas on fostering fresh thinking in such situations, see the "Supplementary Reading" at the end of this chapter.

This desert island exercise specifically avoids the project at hand to remove any constraints, but there is also value in warming up in the same subject area, where some of the suggestions could prove useful. You might do a short warm-up brainstorm focused on difficulties you have had with a related product, for example. Remember, however, that the objective is to get the creative juices flowing rather than for useful output, so keep the problem simple and fun.

If you need more structure to identify numerous risks, try this. Hand out five stickies to each participant. Break the next five minutes into five one-minute cycles. At the start of each cycle, state a question such as "What could go wrong at this point in the schedule?" Then watch and wait while each participant writes one risk on a sticky. Repeat this four more times.

START EARLY—BUT NOT TOO EARLY

As mentioned earlier, there are two opportunities to identify project risks. One is at the beginning of the project (which is the thrust of this chapter). The other is a regular scan for new risks, using a scaled-down version of the process suggested here, as covered in Chapter 8.

As regards your project planning activities, initial risk identification is a chicken-and-egg dilemma. On the one hand, you would like to have the project's risks identified as input to the project planning, since they certainly will affect the budget, schedule, and other plans. In the extreme case, you may decide to cancel or defer the project based on risks you have identified.

On the other hand, you simply will not have enough information to adequately identify project risks until you can present your team with a solid description of the project. Your touchstones for when you have enough information to identify risks are the Product 5Ws and the Process 5Ws listed previously. When you can explain the project to the team in terms of these Ws, the team will be able to identify real risks. Without this detail, they are likely to identify hundreds of imaginary risks, making your risk analysis task in the next step far more difficult.

You may be able to intersperse risk identification and planning activities. For example, you could conduct a preliminary risk identification session using one of the methods below, rather than the schedule-based one, to identify major potential risks. Then you could incorporate them into your initial planning and follow this with a full risk identification session. Also, as explained in Chapter 7, when you make plans to manage your most significant risks, these plans typically require time and money to execute, so you may have to return to your project plans to adjust them then.

Capturing Project Risks

There are several effective ways of discovering risk events. We normally prefer the first one we describe—using the project schedule as a catalyst—but others may work better for you. It depends largely on where you have the strongest information or on the peculiarities of the project at hand. It also depends on the culture of your organization and the nature of your products. Thus, consider your risk identification techniques as the most individualistic part of your risk management process, and experiment accordingly. As your organization gains more experience with risk management, you will find yourself using a variety of techniques due to the uniqueness of each project.

We encourage you to try a few risk-discovery approaches and keep track of those that are effective for you. Use a couple of metrics to track your effectiveness at identifying risks, one relatively short-term one and one of longer range after the project completes. In the short term, estimate the quantity and quality of the risks you identify. This is difficult to do absolutely and quantitatively, because a brainstorming session can generate many ideas of unknown quality. However, if you do use multiple approaches for the same project, tag each risk you find according to the approach you used, and after you have prioritized them, take note of how you discovered the top-ranking ones.

KEY IDEA

After the project's completion, you can form a more accurate picture because you can observe just which risks actually arose and how well you did in predicting them, especially those that proved most significant. If you used two or more methods to discover your risks, backtrack to how you discovered those with the greatest impact. If you missed some significant risks, ask yourself how you might have discovered them in advance.

This project-to-project learning will help you improve your discovery process for future projects.

SCHEDULE BASED

To discover project risks using the schedule, prepare a large version of the schedule (at least a meter—roughly 3 feet) and post it on the wall. This schedule must include all departments with even moderate involvement in the project, and it should also include critical suppliers or other partners. Review this schedule with all participants to ensure that everyone understands and knows how to read it. Figure 4-1 is an illustration of a cross-functional schedule for a small portion of a project in Gantt chart form.

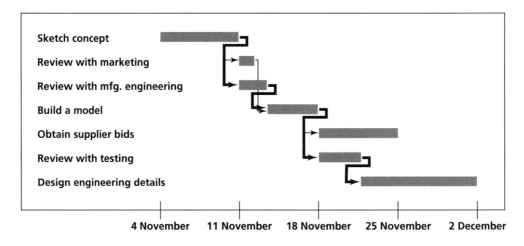

Figure 4-1. Integrated (cross-functional) schedule for a portion of a project in a form suitable for identifying risks. Heavy task connectors denote the critical path.

EXAMPLE Walk through the project week by week or month by month, repeatedly asking the question, "What could go wrong at this point in the project that would prevent us from achieving project success?" Wait while participants write down on stickies each risk event they visualize and its corresponding impact, one risk per sticky. It is essential for the facilitator to emphasize to the team that it describe risk events and impacts using the attributes you learned in Chapters 1 and 2. You will find that it takes practice to develop

KEY IDEA accurate, brief, and clear risk statements. The facilitator and the team

should be referencing the pullout card (in the back of the book) as a checklist to ensure that they have developed solid risk statements.

After the walkthrough, ask participants to post their stickies on the appropriate month of the schedule. This automatically generates a "sticky density" diagram, which is useful itself because it shows you where risk is concentrated in the project. Even if there are duplicates, the density highlights high-risk areas with multiple "votes." (See Chapter 9 for more on sticky density diagrams.)

KEY IDEA

Now consolidate the stickies, eliminating duplicates, and transcribe each risk from its sticky to the spreadsheet or other database you have prepared previously. Note that you will only be entering four fields for each risk now—the risk identifier, risk owner, risk event description, and its impact. You will fill in the other fields as you complete subsequent steps of the process. Do not be surprised when you begin filling in your spreadsheet or database that you are missing some key data. This is normal, and you simply should contact the originator to fill in the missing data.

Some teams, especially in large military development programs, use a similar process based on a work breakdown structure (WBS) organized according to the product's architecture, rather than a schedule. This approach tends to emphasize technical risk to the detriment of schedule risk, so if you do use this approach, also make a conscious effort to catch schedule risks.

DEVELOPMENT PROCESS BASED

This is similar to the schedule-based approach, except that the chart used to prompt the risks is the company's product development process. Seeing as this more generic chart is not project specific, you will have to do an even better job of describing the details of the project so that participants can mentally fill in potential hotspots.

The success of this approach depends greatly on your company having a graphical portrayal of its product development process in a form suitable for this exercise. In general, process charts that work well highlight interactions and coordination between functions, because this is where the risk in a project often resides. Figure 4-2 illustrates such a process chart for a small part of a project. To clarify the contrast between the schedule-based and the process-based approaches, we have included exactly the same activities in both Figures 4-1 and 4-2. That is, these tasks follow this small portion of the company's development process to the letter.

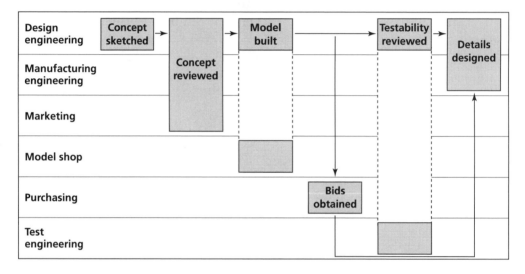

Figure 4-2. Product development process map for the same small part of a project shown in Figure 4-1.

SUCCESS-THWARTING BASED

This method draws directly from the definition of risk: the possibility that an undesired outcome disrupts your project. After you describe the project to the participants, ask them to help you list roughly five characteristics that would describe success for this project. Add a couple more if necessary so that you have a reasonably complete picture of success. Post this list prominently.

KEY IDEA

Now start asking your participants what could go wrong that would keep you from attaining this picture of success. As contributions slow down, and to ensure that you have looked at the project from all angles, prompt them with different facets of the project, perhaps different phases, departments, technologies, or suppliers. Or ask about items that are novel in this project or implicit assumptions that bear consideration.

As the participants suggest risks, list them in brainstorming fashion. (Later you will have to return to these risks to identify their corresponding impacts.) Then transcribe them to your ongoing spreadsheet format. Observe that this approach does not provide a sticky density view of the project that draws your attention to areas of high risk in the project, but you can build something similar by writing each identified risk on a sticky and then building an affinity diagram (i.e., arrange the stickies on a surface until they seem to clump together in natural groups, then name the groups). The large, dense groups suggest parts of the project that are particularly risky so that you can focus more management attention here.

PROMPT-LIST BASED

This approach draws on the fact that, typically, an organization does not learn from its experience, so it keeps confronting similar problems in project after project. To use this method, you need to compile a history of completed projects. Then you review the completed projects one by one, looking for areas in which you repeatedly experience problems or risks. If you conduct the post-project reviews suggested in Chapter 11, you will have this information already. The Ishikawa Risk Model (Chapter 2) may provide a helpful framework for discovering and organizing your risks.

The next step is to build a "prompt list." Such lists are often called checklists, but there is an important difference. A pilot's checklist is typical of a genuine checklist: the pilot goes through every item on the list for every flight to ensure that everything necessary for the flight is acceptable. A prompt list is more open-ended. Nothing on it must be done, but it prompts you to consider things that you might not otherwise. Use a prompt list only to the extent that it helps you.

Once you have your prompt list, you can use it on any future project. Update it as you use it so that it continually becomes more useful. An advantage of this technique is that it can supplement another one, such as the schedule-based technique, as a second check to assure that you have neglected nothing.

Figure 4-3 lists items that may help you build your own prompt list. You can find other lists in many of the resources listed in the "Supplementary Reading" (such as Capers Jones and Carnegie Mellon in this chapter).

Product Definition
- Conflicts with current or planned products
- Clear, stable product definition
- Market need, customer use unclear
- The product's physical environment
- Ergonomics; user friendliness
- Product cost

Development Team
- Project leadership
- Availability of people
- Specific skills needed
- Team geographic/cultural dispersion
- Team training, facilities, equipment, or support
- Project budget

Quality and Legal
- Quality; reliability
- Safety; product liability
- Patent infringement/protection
- Regulatory/environmental regulations

Manufacturing; Outside Resources
- Sourcing; parts availability; supplier quality
- Manufacturing facilities and skills
- Alliances; partners

Technical
- Technology availability/readiness
- Product verification; field testing
- Hardware-software conflicts

Sales and Distribution
- Launch timing
- Product distribution; sales support
- Documentation; training; servicing; maintenance

Figure 4-3. Thought starters for use in creating an organization-specific prompt list.

Please do not use any of these lists as your own prompt list; they are far too general to be of direct value to you. Instead, use them to remind you as you review your projects to create your own organization-specific prompt list. For example, one of the items on the list in Figure 4-3 (the last item in the first group) is product cost. Suppose that certain major components of your products typically fluctuate wildly in price. You would narrow down these items and examine how their price typically varies, then include this specific phenomenon on your prompt list.

A variation on this approach is to find a similar project that you have completed. Then look at its performance in terms of:

- warranty claims,
- customer complaints or service calls,
- actual sales relative to pre-launch forecast, and
- scrap rates and backorder problems.

A discussion of these may prompt risk items for the current project.

Facilitating the Session

Leading a risk identification session is a demanding job. It requires skill in facilitating a diverse audience and drawing out all of its ideas. It also requires a solid understanding of the risk management process in order to keep the ideas on track (for example, to flag suggestions that are issues rather than risks). Finally, the leader must appreciate the novelties of the project being analyzed and keep the group headed in productive directions.

BALANCE BETWEEN OPTIMISM AND PESSIMISM

Some groups detect no problems ahead—or they deny them. Others see a multitude of risks in every task. Neither of these extremes is productive in managing risk, so the facilitator needs to steer the group toward a middle course. We cover these two situations separately, because they require different corrections.

Some action-oriented people, especially managers, operate in the mode that they can handle any adversity when it occurs. Although this may be commendable, it is precisely the style that we are trying to improve upon, because dealing with risks after they occur is both disruptive and expensive. One way to handle this situation is to re-examine some of your recent projects and identify risks that did in fact transpire. Emphasize the loss involved—A$500,000 (Australian) due to this risk, four weeks for that one, and so on. Ask if these risks could have been anticipated, and if so, how they could have been mitigated through early planning. In other words, build a case for proactive risk management in your organization, based on its history in dealing with project risk.

Others identify so many risks that it demoralizes them. We have had managers tell us that they did not want to undertake project risk management, because their people were so pessimistic that they would discourage themselves from even working on the project (perhaps these managers were the "denial type" mentioned above). In this case, try to move on from risk identification quickly into the analysis and planning steps. Once participants see that many risks are minor—and that they can manage the significant ones—they are likely to be comfortable with proceeding. If you have to cut the identification step short to rebuild the team's confidence, make sure that you return to that step soon. In working through the risk steps, however, it may also turn out that pessimism is justified, and the team can make a legitimate case for such overwhelming risk that the project should be terminated, delayed, or allocated a larger budget. Although this may be painful for management to hear, it is better to discover and resolve this issue before investing in such projects.

In either case, the facilitator clearly has an important role in identifying and correcting either of these unproductive trends. This reinforces our suggestion earlier that the team leader may not be the best person to lead a balanced risk identification process.

Running Example

EXAMPLE Here we begin an example that we will build upon as we proceed through the risk management process in the next several chapters to illustrate how the process is applied. If you find this example more comprehensible than absorbing the concepts above, you may wish to begin each following chapter by turning first to this section at its end.

Our example risk is a hypothetical, industry-neutral one that we can all understand. Our subject, Bernardo, is a TV news addict. Based on what he saw on last night's news, he is now concerned about having a heart attack. We will walk through an exercise to determine how likely Bernardo's heart attack is, along with why Bernardo believes he will have a heart attack, possible preventative measures, and finally, what he is going to do in the event of a heart attack despite preventative measures. We use this example because it does not depend on any industry knowledge. Please do not consider it medical advice or suggestive of any particular behavior that one should adopt.

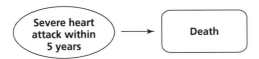

Figure 4-4. To start the running example, we list the risk event and impact statements, which are the primary components of the Standard Risk Model.

Figure 4-4 is the start of the Standard Risk Model that captures the risk event and its impact. The risk event is worded as, "I will have a severe heart attack within the next five years," and Bernardo's impact is worded as, "I will die."

Remember, the risk event answers the question of what event he is concerned about happening and his impact statement should tell him the consequence when the risk event occurs. As you can observe, both of his statements meet their intended purposes. Also, observe that there are other possible impacts, such as being incapacitated, but he focuses on the most severe one.

Summary

This chapter described several techniques you can use to perform the first step of the risk management process, identifying project risks. We covered the need to carefully select a skilled facilitator and described how a brainstorming workshop will generate the initial risk list. We also highlighted some behaviors that can degrade your workshop results, along with some techniques to overcome those behaviors. Next, in Chapter 5, you will shorten and refine your list of risks.

KEY IDEA

Although we have attempted to provide you with the best tools available for identifying risks, please keep in mind that you will never identify all of your project's risks. Some of them are unknowable, and even the best of techniques will overlook some risks. You will have ongoing opportunities later in the project to discover other risks. In short, the objective is to improve your odds greatly, not eliminate all risk.

Supplementary Reading

Jones, Capers. *Assessment and Control of Software Risks*. Englewood Cliffs, New Jersey: Prentice-Hall, 1994. Lists 60 general risks common to software development projects, many of which also apply to hardware development, and devotes about eight pages to discussing each one in a common format. Jones' risks may be helpful in reminding you of risks in your project.

Harvey, Jerry B. *The Abilene Paradox*. San Francisco: Jossey-Bass, 1996. This is a classic collection of essays on organizational behavior. The title one outstandingly illustrates the perils of groupthink and could help prepare participants for a brainstorming session. Also, read, "Captain Asoh and the Concept of Grace" for insights on being straightforward. Both are available as videos.

Kelley, Tom, *The Art of Innovation*. New York: Doubleday, 2001. Whichever risk identification technique you use, you will rely on brainstorming to identify risks. Basic brainstorming rules, as provided in our Chapter 4, are well known. Kelley's Chapter 4 provides advanced brainstorming techniques, as practiced by a leading product development firm.

Rummler, Geary A. and Brache, Alan M. *Improving Performance: How to Manage the White Space on the Organization Chart*. San Francisco: Jossey-Bass, 1995. Excellent source on constructing the type of development process map shown in Figure 4-2 of our book.

Taxonomy-Based Risk Identification. CMU/SEI-93-TR-6, Pittsburgh, Pennsylvania: Carnegie Mellon University, 1993. This 90-page technical report outlines a specific technique for risk identification. Although it is aimed at software development, the technique is generic enough that it can be applied to most product development efforts. The questionnaire documented in the report is an excellent source for probing into potential problem areas in your projects.

5
STEP 2—ANALYZING RISKS

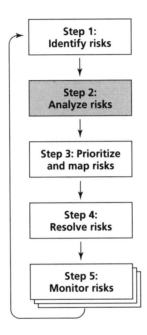

In Chapter 4, you and your team identified and listed a set of risk events and impacts for your project. Your list may be a long one, which is quite normal. Many teams stop here, with their long list of risks, decide they should manage all the risks because they seem serious, but then concentrate on the "real" work of completing the project. Ultimately, even though their intention was sincere, they fail due to previously identified risks that occur throughout the life of the project. We are going to show you new ways of breaking this risk management failure cycle by decomposing your risks into ones that you can manage effectively.

Before starting, we remind you that if you desire concrete examples of this process of analysis, please start the chapter by reading the "Running Example" at the end.

The goal of this step is to understand which risks are significant enough to manage actively as a team. To understand your risks, reconvene the same group used for the risk identification workshop to determine the following information for each risk:

- why you believe the risk event and its impact will occur,
- what the total loss would be if the risk event occurred,
- why you believe the total loss will be that particular amount, and
- the subjective probabilities for the risk event and its impact.

(For a simple project, this workshop can be a continuation of the risk identification workshop, as long as the total session does not exceed two hours.)

To simplify our explanation of risk analysis, we break down each part of the process and describe it in a sequence that facilitates comprehension. However, the actual analysis sequence need not follow the flow of the text. As you gain experience in conducting these workshops, you will discover refinements that work for you. Figure 5-1 outlines a typical sequence of events to follow as you conduct the risk analysis workshop. We prefer this sequence simply because it concentrates attention on a particular risk

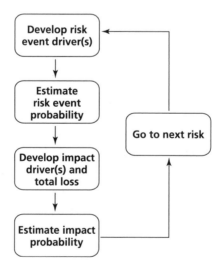

Figure 5-1. This diagram illustrates a typical sequence for analyzing your risks. For ease of explanation, we cover these items in a different order in the text.

event first and completes all factors related to it before changing the focus to this risk's impact. Then the focus moves on to the next risk.

Risk analysis is a critical element of the whole risk management process. If you fail to understand the facts underlying a risk, you will be burdened with risks that have no basis and thus waste the team's time. Performing this analysis requires team members to *justify why* they are concerned about a risk. The risk analysis workshop will not only collect this vital information but also build consensus around the conclusion.

CAUTION

Establish the Facts

During the 1960s, the television show *Dragnet* depicted the stoic life of two Los Angeles detectives. One of those detectives, Joe Friday, was stone cold and strictly business. Sometimes characters would embellish events they had witnessed, and Joe, being the observant professional, would spot these exaggerations and utter, "Just the facts."

During the analysis phase, facilitators should emulate Joe Friday. The key to successful risk management is not managing the risk itself but rather the *facts* leading you to believe risks will occur. We call these facts risk drivers. A risk driver is something *existing* in the project environment that leads you to believe that a particular risk event or impact could occur. For example, if your risk is that a prototype could be delivered late, a driver for this could be that the prototype shop is overloaded making models for a trade show. Drivers are divided into two categories: risk event drivers and impact drivers. Figure 5-2 illustrates how drivers are critical to the Standard Risk Model.

KEY IDEA

Throughout this book, we place great emphasis on understanding and managing your project facts. We believe that these facts are absolutely the key to managing project risk successfully. We find that teams inexperienced with risk management tend to manage the risk itself without understanding the facts that cause it. This lack of understanding usually results in ineffective risk resolution strategies. For an illustration of the critical role of your underlying facts, see the "Running Example" at the end of this chapter and following ones.

In addition to facts that may exist for your present project, your project histories may show some situations that happen so often, or probabilities

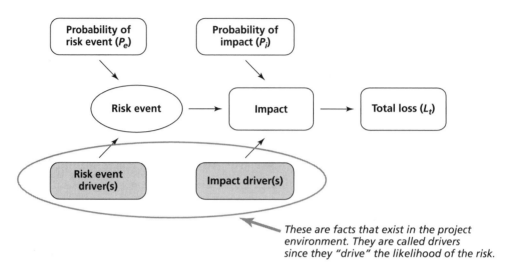

Figure 5-2. Facts determine the likelihood of risks. Risk event drivers influence the risk event and impact drivers do the same for the impact and total loss.

of occurrence that are so well known, you may consider them to be "facts." For instance, let us say that your policy is to have customers review your product specifications. Your history shows that in 9 out of the last 10 projects, the customer added at least one new feature to the specification during this review. Since the customer adds a new feature 90 percent of the time they review the product specifications, we could reasonably assume that this is a "fact" about our project environment.

EXAMPLE

CONDUCTING THE WORKSHOP

You will normally use the same workshop facilitator and setup discussed in Chapter 4 and reconvene the same team that performed your risk identification. This time the facilitator should come prepared by having each risk documented on the spreadsheet (or other risk management tool) along with the following information (as described in Chapter 4):

- risk identifier,
- risk owner,
- risk event, and
- impact.

The workshop's intent is to enable your team to understand which risks are real and why they could have serious consequences for your project. The facilitator will open the workshop with a review of the risk events and impacts you have collected.

This workshop not only helps the team to understand its project better, but also builds the team. Often, project team members do not feel that management or their leaders listen to them effectively or even take them seriously. How many times have we heard, "If they would have only listened to me, we could have prevented that from happening." Now you are giving your team members a chance to be heard and to show that you are going to take action.

The facilitator's role is to guide the group in discovering the drivers contributing to a negative consequence for the project. An experienced facilitator can ask probing questions on the following topics to ensure that all possible sources of risk event drivers and impact drivers are uncovered:

- How well is the project defined?
- How much involvement does the customer have in developing the features and functions that are going to be implemented?
- What is the level of expertise of the engineers who developed the requirements?
- What proposed staffing levels are going to be committed to the project?
- Does everyone understand the product development methodology?
- Is the product development team experienced with any new technologies being introduced?
- Is the management team experienced in managing the complexity of this particular project?
- What trends are occurring in the marketplace?
- How are suppliers going to be integrated in this project?
- Are there any weak lines of communication?

Notice that these questions are similar to some suggested in Chapter 4, but the difference is in what they seek to uncover. In Chapter 4, you were looking for risk events and their impacts. Here, you delve deeper to ask what facts are the cause of a certain risk and determine its magnitude.

DEVELOPING RISK EVENT DRIVERS

Referring to Figure 5-3, the Standard Risk Model, we first determine the risk event drivers. These drivers are the *facts* leading you to believe the risk event is imminent. After determining the risk event drivers, we move on to development of the impact drivers, and finally to quantifying total loss, in the next sections.

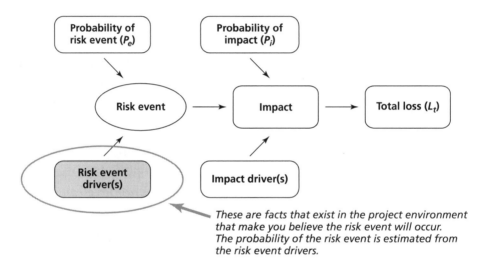

Figure 5-3. Risk event drivers are facts in the project environment that determine the likelihood of the risk event.

KEY IDEA

The facilitator must ascertain why the originator of the risk event thought it was important. Frequently, you will find that team members assume everyone else knows what they know. But as you will discover, others in the group often are unaware that certain drivers lead to serious risks.

When you first apply risk management, you will likely find that the team relies heavily on the facilitator to assist in developing the risk drivers. The facilitator must use a variety of techniques to get the information out into the open. One of our favorites is the "George Patton Tactic." When a field commander would make a statement or comment without any supporting facts to General George S. Patton, he would fire back, "How do we know this?" The commander was forced to be better prepared next time he made a statement or comment.

Consider an example of the Patton technique. During the risk identifica- EXAMPLE tion workshop, a systems engineer has listed a risk event: "The development team will not attend the system requirements review." The facilitator, seeing that someone is potentially going to start some finger pointing, quickly comes back to the systems engineer and asks, "How do we know this?" This requires the systems engineer to articulate her case and present *facts* supporting her belief that the development team will be unable to attend the review. It may turn out that your systems engineer was new to your company, and she assumed that development teams always have poor attendance records at reviews because that was the case at her last company. In this instance, we probably do not have a risk that warrants active management.

Now consider the same risk but with a different risk event driver. In this case, the systems engineer stated that on the last seven projects, the development team attended only one system requirements review. Now you would have high confidence that this is a legitimate risk that merits your attention. When we demonstrate how to estimate the probability of the risk event and impact, you will see how the drivers are used to develop probabilities.

The facilitator should also be the quality control monitor to verify that the risk event drivers clearly but briefly answer the question, "What are the project facts leading you to believe this risk event will occur?" We have also found it essential to have a recorder who can enter the driver statements in real time into the spreadsheet. Do not require the facilitator to record the data, since this will detract from his or her primary duty of guiding the entire workshop.

CAUTION

DEVELOPING IMPACT DRIVERS

For each risk event identified by the team, the facilitator ensured that a risk event driver existed that would lead you to believe the risk would occur. Now we focus on the impact drivers. Figure 5-4 illustrates how the impact drivers fit into the Standard Risk Model.

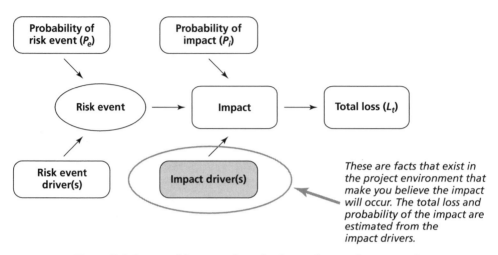

Figure 5-4. Impact drivers are facts in the project environment that establish the impact's likelihood, given that the risk event occurs.

Impact drivers answer two important questions:

- What project facts make the impact more or less likely to occur?
- What project facts establish the magnitude of the total loss?

The impact is the *consequence* that could result if the risk event occurred. Notice that a probability exists for the consequence. Just because the risk event occurs does not necessarily mean the consequence will occur. For instance, you may state that if you miss the ship date for your product going to Japan, it will result in a seven-day delay in delivery to the customer. In this example, you should determine why you would have a seven-day delay. The first impact driver may be, "The weight of our product dictates we must ship by boat." The second impact driver may be, "If the shipping date is missed, the shipping broker will need to redo the paperwork, renegotiate the shipping, and find a new vessel, all of which will take one week." The point is that you had to justify why the delay is seven days and how confident you were in the seven days, and you did that by documenting the impact drivers.

QUANTIFYING TOTAL LOSS

As the risk analysis continues, you move on to quantify the total loss. The total loss is the magnitude of the loss value accrued when a risk event occurs. Many people are confused over the difference between the impact and the total loss. The impact is simply a statement such as, "the delivery date will slip by 15 workdays." Fifteen workdays is the total loss, which is actually part of the impact. We prefer to measure that loss in time or money (ideally, we like to see all losses converted into time using the cost of delay, as discussed in Chapter 7). Other quantities could be used, such as performance or quality measures, but when your organization is focused on time, schedule slippage is a natural measure. Whatever you select, we recommend consistently using one unit—for instance, either workdays *or* Canadian dollars—throughout a project so you can compare risks easily.

The facilitator can also help the team derive the total loss. On the surface, this appears to be straightforward. However, you are likely to find that many people hold differing views on the value of the total loss. This is precisely why developing solid impact drivers is important. Your facilitator needs to be aware of the length of time being spent to make these quantifications. If you are spending too much time in the workshop trying to develop the total loss value, you probably have not done a good enough job of developing well-written impact drivers. The facilitator should guide the team back to revisit the quality of the impact drivers.

CAUTION

Throughout the risk analysis workshops, you will find that some total losses can be derived by simply totaling the duration of each process step contributing to the impact. For instance, assume your risk event is a hardware defect that results in an impact requiring you to create a new circuit board. Since the impact is the creation of a new circuit board, you need to know the total loss of that impact. There are discrete process steps you will need to take to create the circuit board, and those steps will have known durations. Simply add up the length of process steps to obtain the total loss for creating a new circuit board.

EXAMPLE

Here is another circumstance that may occur. A risk may be on the critical path of your project, and someone may state, "I cannot tell what the total loss will be but I know that we will experience a day-for-day slip if this occurs." If you *truly* cannot determine the total loss, and the risk is on the critical path, then you must treat this as a special case, recognizing that the reason for doing the analysis is to be able to prioritize your risks and commit the most serious ones to active management. For this risk, you will not have a total loss or expected loss, and you will not prioritize it. You simply skip these steps and flag this risk for active management, regardless of how the other risks rank. If you have solid impact drivers, you will not have to use this special treatment often.

At this point in the risk analysis workshop, the facilitator has guided your team through the development of risk event drivers, impact drivers, and the total loss for each risk that was identified in the previous workshop. This information should now be recorded on your spreadsheet or a similar tool. Refer to Chapter 9 to see how risk data can be represented in a spreadsheet.

RISK SCALING CONSIDERATIONS

Before moving on to risk calculations, we consider the scaling systems used to represent total loss. Should you use quantitative or qualitative data? We have used a variety of techniques to represent the magnitude of total loss on various product development projects, and we usually come back to using time to quantify total loss. However, here are some additional units you can use to determine the total loss of your project risks:

- Numerical units (quantitative)
  - workdays (our preferred choice)
  - calendar days
  - financial (Australian dollars, yen, euros)
  - staff months
- Subjective units (qualitative)
  - minimal, very low, moderate, high, critical
  - low, medium, high
  - 1, 2, 3, 4, 5

In the previous section, we reviewed our preferred approach and explained how to use the numerical units of workdays. Our experience in product development has taught us the need to keep things simple, and since everyone can relate to time and it is easy to measure, it naturally becomes the preferred choice. In addition, quantitative data typically is easier to use than qualitative data, which is often ambiguous. However, sometimes you will find that developing quantitative data is difficult and you will ultimately need to make an educated guess on the values. Those who are untrained in risk management, seeing your numbers, may get a false sense of security due to the apparent accuracy in the quantitative data; for example, stating 0.7 when you know only that a value is somewhere between 0.6 and 0.8.

CAUTION

We use workdays instead of just "days" because the latter is ambiguous. For instance, people might say that a schedule slips three weeks. Do they mean 21 calendar days or 15 workdays? The problem comes into play when you start to compare risks; if the scales for the total loss being used are not defined, you cannot prioritize your risks effectively. Similarly, if you use monetary terms, not only should all risks be expressed in the same currency, but they should also relate to the same financial quantity: unit manufacturing cost, project expense, or revenue contribution, for example. (To reinforce the lesson to be specific on currencies, we specify in our examples just which kind of dollars we intend, because several countries use dollars for their currency, or we avoid dollars altogether. The important point is to pick a numerical unit and stick to it.)

Instead of using a quantitative scale for total loss, some may chose to use a qualitative scaling system, with labels such as low, medium, and high impact, which is attractive due to its simplicity; however, you have to provide descriptions of what each point on the scale represents. For instance, to a manufacturing engineer, any risks that can reduce production throughput on the manufacturing line will usually be considered a high loss, while a software engineer may consider the same risk to be low. Without descriptive labels on the scale, the severity of a loss becomes relative depending on one's point of view.

KEY IDEA

If you have used labels such as "quite unlikely" (for risk likelihood) or "seriously late" (for total loss), then you have established a qualitative scale (known more formally as an ordinal scale). Even if you define these labels carefully, qualitative scales have several difficulties that make working with them problematic:

- Each individual is likely to interpret descriptions of each category differently.

- Error enters in borderline cases that do not fit well in any category.
- Mathematical operations, such as calculating expected loss, cannot be performed on qualitative scales, since the space between labels is generally unknown.

Conrow (see "Supplementary Reading") discusses the complications of working with qualitative scales in detail, and describes how to work with them.

Calculate the Risk

It is amazing how often we have been in project meetings where participants have not been trained in risk management, and someone states "This sure is risky." We always like to probe that statement by asking, "What does that mean, 'risky'?" The person will typically stare at us bewildered because he or she inherently knows something is "risky" but cannot express it in words. Here we describe some simple ways to determine just how "risky" something is.

To understand the seriousness of a risk you must know the probability of the risk event and the probability of its impact, which, together, we call its likelihood. In addition, you must know the total loss that could be realized if the risk materialized. We have discovered that most of the probabilities will usually be of a subjective, not objective, nature. Many different techniques have been developed over the years in various industries to estimate probabilities. Our goal is to keep this process simple, but let us be frank: the techniques used to develop most probability estimates on a project are subjective and therefore are only guesses. However, you can make them *educated* guesses by using the information you already have on hand—the risk event and impact drivers.

One of the biggest problems teams face in risk management is their desire to be very precise in their probability estimates. However, they have lost sight of the fact they are dealing with subjective probabilities and so precision need not extend to the fifth decimal place. It is the facilitator's role to ensure that the team does not spend an excessive amount of time fine-tuning probability estimates.

PROBABILITY ESTIMATION TECHNIQUES

Using drivers of the risk event and impact to guide you, you next assign a probability, usually a subjective one, to the risk event and the impact of each risk. Although we have used different techniques when developing the probability estimates, we usually rely on group consensus, individual assignments, or wideband Delphi (described below). In addition, we usually prefer to do the estimates during the risk analysis workshop, with the entire team present. Team dynamics and risk complexity are prime considerations when selecting which techniques to pursue. Often we actually use all three techniques on a project. For instance, most risk probability estimates can be determined using group consensus. However, you will find some risks are either controversial or complex, and it may be better to use wideband Delphi. When you have a mature team that works well together, we have found it best to use group consensus due to the speed it brings to the process.

Our first technique, group consensus, is to have the facilitator simply walk through each risk event and impact and ask the group to estimate the probabilities. If your development team is experienced and your drivers well written, you will usually be able to provide estimates quickly. These estimates will also be easier for the team to make if you obtain them just after you have developed the drivers.

For the second technique, individual assignments, the facilitator assigns certain participants to develop the probabilities for a risk. We usually use this approach when the session has continued for a long while, and we've decided to stop for the day and bring the team back together later to review the data. However, we have found the quality of the probability estimates are not as good as compared to the group consensus approach, so be prepared when you reconvene to rework some of the estimates.

The third technique, wideband Delphi, is especially effective in developing probability estimates. However, its downside is that it usually increases the length of time to develop the estimates, and as risk analysis workshops become longer, data quality decreases correspondingly. The wideband Delphi technique is similar to the group consensus with the exception that each team member anonymously votes for his or her probability estimate, and the facilitator collects the votes and then records each one on a flipchart or whiteboard. If all agree on the estimate, use it, but usually estimates will vary and another round of voting will be needed. As you can see, if the team has a fairly large number of risks to analyze, it can take a long time to develop a complete set of probability estimates using wideband Delphi.

CAUTION

This technique provides a valuable sanity check on your risk data. When the facilitator writes the estimates on the whiteboard, the entire team can see if they are converging. If the estimates are very close, you can safely assume your risk driver data is solid. However, if the estimates differ greatly, then usually someone knows something that other team members do not, so there may be a missing risk driver. The facilitator should key in on finding additional drivers if estimates vary greatly.

CAUTION

By the way, the primary reason the voting is anonymous is to prevent an effect called groupthink. Groupthink occurs when a team is so concerned with being united they fail to recognize other alternatives and options and end up making poor decisions (see *The Abilene Paradox* in the "Supplementary Reading" in Chapter 4 for more on this). A strong or highly respected team leader can accelerate this effect because team members will go along readily with that leader's viewpoint.

ESTIMATE RISK EVENT PROBABILITY

KEY IDEA

Referring to the Standard Risk Model, you estimate the probability of the risk event using one of the three estimation techniques just discussed. The facilitator guides the team through the risk event, and depending on which technique you are using, the team collectively establishes a probability estimate based upon the risk event drivers. As you do this, it is crucial for your team to remember that probability estimates are *not* based on the risk events themselves but rather on the risk event *drivers*—the facts that tell you why the risk event will occur. If your team has not documented any risk event drivers, then the probability of the risk in question is so low that you should move onto the next risk event.

Our experience has shown that you should limit the number of your probability options. We recommend you use the following discrete values:

- If there is no chance of occurrence use 0 percent.

- If greater than 0 percent but less than 20.5 percent use 10 percent.
- If equal to or greater than 20.5 percent but less than 40.5 percent use 30 percent.
- If equal to or greater than 40.5 percent but less than 60.5 percent use 50 percent.
- If equal to or greater than 60.5 percent but less than 80.5 percent use 70 percent.
- If equal to or greater than 80.5 percent but less than 100 percent use 90 percent.

We limit the team's options primarily due to the tendency of teams to argue over the probability estimates; even experienced teams need to be reminded that they are usually dealing with subjective, not objective, probability. We can recall one product development team that had a heated debate over whether the probability was 23 or 25 percent! After that particular workshop, we modified our risk analysis process to use discrete values. If you find that you have many low-probability, high-impact risks, then you might instead use more of a logarithmic scale: 90, 50, 20, 10, 5, 2, 1 percent. In either case, the point is to limit the choices to about a half dozen discrete values.

A word of caution: if someone tries to label a risk event with a probability of 100 percent, then it is certain and it is therefore not a risk but an issue that may need your immediate attention (see the "Uncertainty" section in Chapter 1 for more on distinguishing issues from risks).

CAUTION

ESTIMATE RISK IMPACT PROBABILITY

The facilitator guides the team in developing a probability estimate for the impact using one of the three previously mentioned techniques. As before, base the estimate on the impact drivers, not the impact itself. The facilitator will review the impact and the impact drivers and work with the team to develop the probability estimate.

Again, limit your probability scale. We recommend you use the discrete values listed for the risk event probability, with the addition of being able to select 100 percent. We add 100 percent as an option because it is entirely possible for the probability of the *impact* to be a certainty. For example, if you were a politician running for re-election, your risk event is not getting enough votes to beat your competitor, and your impact will be the loss of the election. If you do not get enough votes, there is a 100 percent chance you will lose the election.

CALCULATE EXPECTED LOSS

Now you are to the final, easy step of answering that popular question, "How risky is it?" Use the probabilities of the risk event and impact along with the total loss to calculate the expected loss. Expected loss is the average loss you can expect from the risk. Figure 5-5 illustrates the equation and the individual terms used in it.

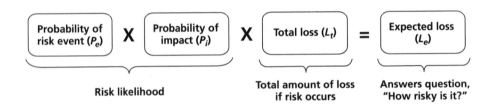

Figure 5-5. Factors entering into calculating expected loss, which is the prime criterion for prioritizing risks.

Here is how this would all tie together in an example. Assume we have estimated that there is a 50 percent (probability of risk event) chance that a plastic injection tool will be two weeks late (risk event), and it will delay our next production build by two weeks, which has a 70 percent (probability of impact) chance of delaying the project, resulting in €500,000 (total loss, in euros) lost profit (impact). Therefore, P_e = 50 percent, P_i = 70 percent and, L_t = €500,000. Plugging in the numbers into the Figure 5-5 equation, the expected loss for this risk is €175,000. This means that, *on average*, this risk is going to cost the company €175,000 in lost profit. If the production build is actually delayed and this delays the project the entire two weeks, the loss will be the full €500,000. But this is scaled down on average, because the tool is only 50 percent likely to be delayed, and there is only a 70 percent chance that a late tool will delay final product delivery. If you are expressing your losses in monetary terms, as we did here, expected loss is identical to expected monetary value (EMV), which some companies use.

Of all of the quantities we have just introduced, expected loss is the central one because it is your primary means, going forward, of comparing and prioritizing various identified risks. It is the main criterion you will use to decide to actively manage some risks and let others remain dormant.

KEY IDEA

Working with Differing Units and Qualitative Scales

Although we advise using the same quantitative scale to express total loss for all risks on a project, sometimes you will be unable to use a common scale or to express all risks quantitatively. If you cannot express the total loss numerically, one approach is to define your labels, such as "medium," as specifically as possible by calibrating them. Table 5-1 shows how you can calibrate a label when it means different things for different project objectives. If you construct a table such as this, make sure you perform some cross checks on it.

CAUTION

Table 5-1. Calibration values for total loss when using qualitative scales.

Total loss	Schedule slip (workdays)	Target product cost overrun (Swiss francs)	Project budget overrun (Swiss francs)	Product performance (throughput, units/minute)
None	0	0	0	220
Low	1–5	<0.50	<150,000	205
Medium	6–15	0.50–1.20	150,000–500,000	190
High	>15	>1.20	>500,000	180

For example, the schedule slip column and the project budget overrun column together imply a cost-of-delay value—that is, the amount of budget overrun that you would trade for a day of delay. In the row for the "low" label, you see that you are deeming a midpoint of three days of delay is equal to a midpoint of SF75,000 (Swiss francs) of expense, which implies a cost of delay of SF25,000/day. Is this reasonable? If you do the same for the "medium" and "high" rows, you get SF31,000/day and SF33,000/day, respectively. Are all of these reasonably consistent? You can make many other similar quick checks to ascertain that you indeed have a robust, consistent set of labels. In Chapter 7's "Supplementary Reading," we list a source for calculating these trade-off values between the objectives of your project, and these calculated trade-off values will give you something else to check against.

A slightly different approach is to use consequence factors. A consequence factor is a (dimensionless) value between zero and one. You establish consequence factor values by building a table that allows you to look up consequence factors for each of the units you are using in assessing project risks. Table 5-2 illustrates such a table for a project in which some risks are expressed in workdays and others in euros. By converting the low-medium-high values in Table 5-1 to numbers in the zero-to-one range, and perhaps adding a few more levels, this table could also be a consequence factor table.

Table 5-2. Consequence factor table.

Monetary total loss if loss is between:	Time total loss if loss is between:	Consequence Factor
€1,000 and €55,000	0.5 and 5.5 workdays	0.1
€56,000 and €105,000	5.6 and 10.5 workdays	0.3
€106,000 and €155,000	10.6 and 15.5 workdays	0.5
€156,000 and €205,000	15.6 and 20.5 workdays	0.7
> €205,000	> 20.5 workdays	0.9
Cost of Delay = €10,000 per workday.		

A consequence factor table represents both a boon and a bane to the team. Once you have one, it establishes consensus among members—and, hopefully, with management—about the trade-off rules that are implicit in the project. For example, Table 5-2 is built on the basis that each workday is worth €10,000, which is what we call the cost of delay. This value, once you know it for your project, is valuable far beyond risk management for making daily decisions regarding "buying" time effectively and consistently. Likewise, a consequence factor table highlights inconsistencies. For instance, one team calculated the cost of delay for their project from the sales they would lose if they were late to market. Then they independently constructed a consequence factor table that greatly undervalued time relative to money according to their cost of delay calculation. When the discrepancy was pointed out, they—and management—were able to reconcile the two and reach a consensus that prevented many future arguments.

The difficulty in building a consequence factor table is precisely that it takes considerable work to reach consensus on equivalent values. These values are project-specific, and arriving at them is called "calibrating the risk model." You must do the calibration to relate all of the units (for instance, euros and workdays) that the team will use as measures of total loss. As we suggested for probabilities, select about five discrete values to use for consequence factors so that the team does not waste time arguing over small differences.

To calculate expected loss, simply replace the total loss, L_t, with the consequence factor in the equation shown in Figure 5-5. Now your risks with different total loss units can be compared quantitatively. One outcome you should be aware of when using consequence factors is that you "weight" all risks equally when they are on the high end of the severity scale. For instance, referring to Table 5-2, a risk with a total loss of €1,000,000 will have the same consequence factor, 0.9, as a risk of €5,000,000. Usually this does not cause a problem if the table is calibrated correctly because, even if you were using regular expected loss calculations, those high-severity risks would have had high expected loss values and thus would be actively managed. In fact, this is an advantage of using consequence factors, because you can avoid arguments over whether a particularly severe risk has a total loss of €1,000,000 or €5,000,000. In reality, this difference does not matter, because either one will be ranked for active management anyway.

We offer one last warning about consequence factors. Just because you have expressed consequences by using numbers now, you still do not have all the attributes of a quantitative scale, which means that, in principle, you should not be performing arithmetic with consequence factors unless you have been careful to calibrate them to be proportional (in what is called a ratio scale). In practice, if your scales are reasonably proportional, the distortion introduced in using consequence factors to calculate expected loss should not greatly affect your risk prioritization. You can

CAUTION

also sidestep this difficulty by using a risk map (see Chapter 6) to decide which risks to manage actively.

Using consequence factors does increase the complexity of your risk analysis, which is the primary reason we advocate using a single total loss unit. We have seen teams get mired down due to the extra work of developing consequence factors, when they should be focusing on developing and implementing risk resolution strategies. If you lose perspective, frustration may set in and disrupt your entire risk management process.

Running Example

EXAMPLE Here we continue the single example that will build as we proceed through the risk management process to illustrate how the process is applied. This hypothetical example is meant only to illustrate the risk management techniques described in this book. We do not intend that anyone use this example as a medical reference or modify any personal behavior based on this data.

In the last chapter, Bernardo had identified a risk of having a heart attack, the impact of which could be death. At present, he has no facts to back up this idea, so his task now is to assemble and analyze his facts (drivers) to assess how serious this risk might be. Once he has completed his analysis in this chapter, he will proceed in later chapters to compare this heart attack risk against other possible risks, and then decide what, if anything, he will do about the risks.

In Figure 5-6, the Standard Risk Model captures the risk event and its impact along with three new additions: risk event drivers, impact drivers, and total loss. The risk event drivers tell Bernardo why he might have a heart attack in the next five years. The risk event drivers are facts about Bernardo in this example. He is a 50-year-old male with a stressful job, does not get regular exercise, is excessively overweight, and has high blood pressure. His impact drivers tell him why he believes he will die at a loss of US$1,500,000. He lives 50 miles from the ambulance, he lives 100 miles from the hospital, his spouse does not drive, and he plans to continue making US$100,000 a year until he retires at age 65. The last driver is key because it allows him to develop the total loss quantitatively. If the heart attack occurred today, he would lose 15 years of salary, which would total US$1,500,000—his total loss.

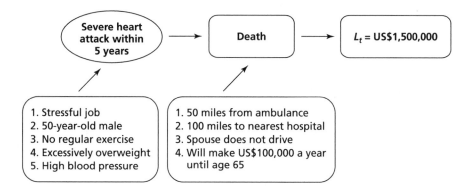

Figure 5-6. Heart attack example, including the risk event drivers and impact drivers, along with the total loss.

Figure 5-7 includes the probabilities for the risk event and impact. He developed the probabilities from the driver information. He estimates that he has a 50 percent chance of having a heart attack in the next five years and a 70 percent chance of dying if he does have a heart attack, and thus

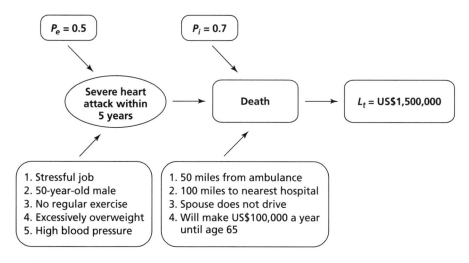

Figure 5-7. Heart attack example with the probabilities of the risk event and impact added.
Source: Adapted from Fastrak Training Inc. Used with permission. ©1995.

of his family losing US$1,500,000 in salary. Although these probabilities are, in the end, subjective judgments, they are based on as many facts (drivers) as he can gather and understand. They are not just plausible guesses. For example, to construct this "Running Example," we estimated the heart-attack probabilities by consulting an emergency medicine physician and by checking some medical information available on the Internet. To give you an idea of the level of detail we explored, we learned that, in the event of cardiac arrest, survival depends strongly on the elapsed time from onset to defibrillation, which is measured in minutes. Thus, distance to the nearest defibrillation capability (for example, an ambulance dispatch facility) is a strong driver. Please remember that, even with the level of detail provided here, this remains generic information and should not be considered medical advice for any individual.

Now Bernardo has the following information: P_e = 50 percent, P_i = 70 percent, and L_t = US$1,500,000. With these terms in the expected loss equation: $P_e \times P_i \times L_t = L_e$, the result is

50 percent $\times$ 70 percent $\times$ US$1,500,000 = US$525,000

As you can see, in this example, fact-based drivers for the risk event and impact provide Bernardo with essential information for making an educated guess on the probabilities of having a heart attack and dying from it. In addition, he put a quantified value—the expected loss—on the risk at US$525,000. Interestingly, Bernardo will never lose US$525,000, but rather US$1,500,000 if he dies, and nothing if he does not. The significance of the expected loss is that it provides a balance between zero and US$1,500,000 based on the probabilities of the two outcomes. This "balanced" value is a single measure of this risk's magnitude that we use in the next chapter to prioritize risks.

Summary

In summary, this chapter described how to develop the drivers that lead you to believe that risk events and impacts will occur. We explained how to use a risk analysis workshop to develop probability estimates for the risk event and impact, and how to calculate the expected loss of a risk.

Going into the next chapter, we will show you how to take the expected loss information for each risk and use it to select and prioritize the risks that your project team will manage.

Supplementary Reading

Conrow, Edmond H. *Effective Risk Management.* Reston, Virginia: American Institute of Aeronautics and Astronautics, 2000. This book is oriented toward very large military and aerospace projects, but it provides considerable information on using (and abusing) qualitative (ordinal) scales in prioritizing risks. See Appendices G and I and pages 144–160, 205–214.

Kerzner, Harold. *Project Management*, Seventh Edition. New York: John Wiley & Sons, Inc., 2001. Chapter 17 provides detailed information on using scales to analyze risks.

Axelrod, Alan, *Patton on Leadership: Strategic Lessons for Corporate Warfare.* Paramus, New Jersey: Prentice Hall Press, 1999. Shows facilitators or team leaders how to demand the facts that lead to useful risk event and impact drivers.

6
STEP 3—PRIORITIZING AND MAPPING RISKS

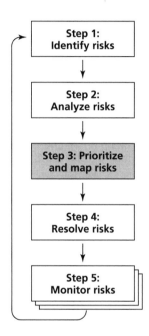

Our goal in this chapter is to identify the most important risks so that the next chapter's action planning efforts can be aimed at them. As risks are identified, some teams may feel overwhelmed by the sheer number of risks that were identified in the workshops. After completing the risk analysis process, this concern usually deepens even more because now facts have been established for the project's risks, which makes their importance even clearer. This chapter imposes order on the list of risks the team will be managing by helping them to address only those that pose the greatest threat to the project's goals.

To illustrate this point, assume for the moment that the product development team has 10 members. After completing the risk identification and analysis workshops, each member has identified 10 risks—a reasonable number at the identification step. However, this means that they would now have 100 risks going forward. These could consume a significant amount of the team's time, considering, for example, that a typical action plan to resolve a single risk could entail developing an alternative design or engaging a contractor having a skill not available in-house. Clearly, we need a way to determine which risks are worthy of the team's active effort and which risks they can simply monitor with minimal effort. By prioritizing risks, the team can focus its attention to its greatest advantage.

How to Prioritize

In the previous chapter, you calculated an expected loss value for each risk, a measure of that risk's overall severity. Using these expected loss values, you can rank your risks in descending order in a spreadsheet. Keep in mind that risk data developed in the workshops are subjective, so some inaccuracies may exist in the probability or total loss estimates that determine the expected loss. In addition, some risks may be special cases due to their catastrophic nature. Therefore, team members will need to apply their expert opinions and reach agreement on which risks to manage. Using a combination of a tool called the risk map (described in this chapter) and group consensus or wideband Delphi techniques (a more structured form of consensus building described in Chapter 5), the team will select the risks they will actively manage. Figure 6-1 outlines the steps that lead progressively to a prioritized list of risks.

1. SORT RISKS BY EXPECTED LOSS

We have emphasized quantifying both the total loss and the risk likelihood for each risk (see the Glossary for definitions of these terms). If you have done this successfully, you will have an absolute ranking for these two quantities and will be able to calculate each risk's expected loss and compare various risks straightforwardly. Using a spreadsheet (or similar tool), the project manager can sort the risks by using the values of expected loss calculated in Chapter 5.

Figure 6-1. This diagram illustrates the steps for prioritizing your risk list.

Table 6-1 shows an example of your risk list after sorting on expected loss. To keep this example simple, we only display a total of 10 risks; however, on your actual projects the number of risks analyzed during this phase may be much higher. The first column will become the priority for each risk. Do not include this column when sorting the data, since it will be used to rank the priority for the entire risk list after you have completed the sorting. The third column will signify the status of the risk (covered later).

If you have decided to express total loss for some risks in other terms, such as money, you will need to construct a separate spreadsheet for them because you cannot mix different expected value quantities. This is an inherent weakness in using expected loss as the sole criterion for prioritizing. Using qualitative scales can help overcome this weakness, but these scales have their own flaws, which were outlined in Chapter 5. The "Supplementary Reading" suggests other means of combining different quantities.

Table 6-1. The project manager integrates risk data that was developed during the risk analysis workshop to rank the risks relatively.

Priority	Risk Identifier	Status	Probability of Risk Event (P_e)	Probability of Impact (P_i)	Likelihood (P_e x P_i)	Total Loss in Workdays (L_t)	Expected Loss (P_e x P_i x L_t = L_e)
1	R16		0.9	1	0.9	22	19.8
2	R1		0.7	0.9	0.63	25	15.8
3	R13		0.9	0.9	0.81	17	13.8
4	R5		0.5	0.9	0.45	22	9.9
5	R2		0.7	0.7	0.49	15	7.4
6	R4		0.7	0.9	0.63	5	3.2
7	R18		0.3	0.9	0.27	10	2.7
8	R7		0.3	0.7	0.21	13	2.7
9	R10		0.1	0.5	0.05	25	1.3
10	R9		0.3	0.5	0.15	4	0.6

Initially you will rank order simply based upon the expected loss.

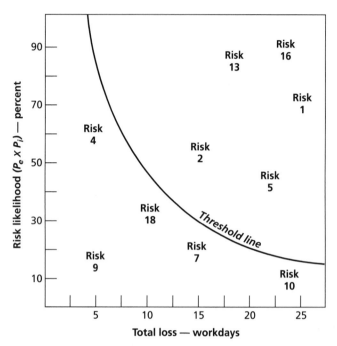

Repeat of Figure 3-3. A risk map showing risks 1, 2, 5, 13, and 16 under active management and five more monitored candidates.

2. DEVELOP A RISK MAP

We introduced the risk map in Figure 3-3, and repeat it here for the reader's convenience. This graph, used broadly in the risk management field, displays risks plotted against total loss on the x-axis and risk likelihood ($P_e \times P_i$) on the y-axis (some people prefer to interchange the two axes). We have shown our axes with numbered scales; however, some may choose to use qualitative labels such as low, medium, and high. We prefer to use quantitative scales because they are straightforward in generating numbers, especially if you have been successful in calculating or translating all of your impacts to a *single* quantity (such as workdays or Canadian dollars of lost profit). If you use numbers, the scales need not be linear. For example, a logarithmic scale on either or both axes may be better for showing areas of high total loss or low risk likelihood.

Once you have the two axes of your risk map well calibrated (refer to Chapter 5. "Working with Differing Units and Qualitative Scales," for a

description of calibration), you can locate the risks you have analyzed. Individual risks should be identified uniquely using your risk identifiers.

This leaves one element of the risk map to mention, the curved threshold line. This is a line of constant expected loss. It divides the risks that you will manage actively—those above the threshold line—from the ones that will not be managed—those below the threshold line.

Your risk quantification scheme determines the shape of this line. If you have been successful in quantifying all risks on a single scale (such as workdays), you can plot this line easily from the formula $P = P_e \times P_i = L_e / L_t$, where L_e is your chosen level of expected loss (discussed in the following paragraphs). If you use a qualitative scale for different objectives, as shown in Table 5-1 (also repeated, below), you will have to calculate the threshold curve similarly from the quantities, or midpoints of ranges, shown in the

Repeat of Table 5-1. Calibration values for total loss when using qualitative scales.

Total loss	Schedule slip (workdays)	Target product cost overrun (Swiss francs)	Project budget overrun (Swiss francs)	Product performance (throughput, units/minute)
None	0	0	0	220
Low	1–5	<0.50	<150,000	205
Medium	6–15	0.50–1.20	150,000–500,000	190
High	>15	>1.20	>500,000	180

table. If possible, calculate the curve for each objective (each column in the table), and then draw an average threshold line considering the various curves you will get from each column in the table. Clearly, this is not an exact process, but if you have been diligent in setting scales for total loss you should obtain a satisfactory result.

Once you have shaped your threshold line, you locate it according to your tolerance for risk, as shown in Figure 6-2. If you can tolerate a higher expected loss, your threshold line moves up higher, and you have fewer risks above it that you will have to manage. As mentioned in Chapter 1, risk management always involves a trade-off in effort because you will never be able to afford to manage all project risks.

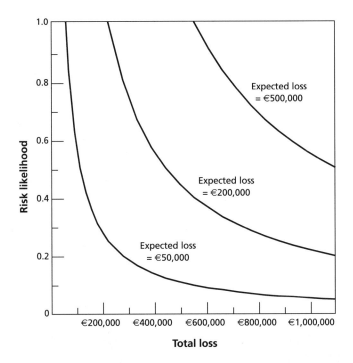

Figure 6-2. Risk map showing three levels at which the threshold for managing risks could be set. The lower the threshold, the more risks are captured for active management, but also the more effort and cost you will expend in managing them.

Consequently, the curve's location should stem from explicitly considering the trade-off between managing too few risks—thus opening the door for downstream project surprises—and managing too many—which will consume project resources that could be put to use on tangible project deliverables.

KEY IDEA

Setting the level of the threshold curve is akin to buying insurance, and this is a helpful way of considering it. You can pay more for higher insurance coverage (a lower threshold line), but then the premiums you pay will cut into other, perhaps more productive or enjoyable, ways you could spend this money. From this viewpoint, there are two ways of setting the level of the threshold line. One is to consider quantitatively the trade-off between the risk protection you obtain and the "premiums" you will pay for it; that is, look at it as a cost-benefit trade-off. The other way of setting the level (often done tacitly when buying insurance) is to set the threshold at a level that is comfortable when considered from either side—the side of not getting enough protection or the side of paying too much to manage risks.

Because setting the threshold line (or deciding just how many risks are on the top 10 list) involves the organization's tolerance for risk, you might work with the stakeholders of your projects to establish the organization's criteria for setting this level. You could specify that you will manage any risks above a certain expected loss, and this expected loss could be relative to the project's size (for monetary expected losses) or urgency (for time-based expected losses). Or you could set the criterion in terms of cost-benefit ratio (see the risk reduction leverage formula in the next chapter).

KEY IDEA

We recognize that establishing both the shape and level of the threshold line will take some work. However, please keep two thoughts in mind as you consider this step. First, you only have to do this once per project; once you establish the curve for a project, it normally remains fixed for that project. Second, this is a very important judgment for a project and it should not be left to chance. Unless you explicitly consider the level at which you will manage your project's risks, you are likely to devote either far too much or far too little effort to them—most likely the latter. Or you will manage them inconsistently, both wasting resources on ineffective risk management of some risks and exposing your project to needless risk on others.

In general, you will manage the risks above the threshold curve and not manage the risks below it. There are two exceptions, however—at the two ends of the total loss spectrum (see Figure 6-3). At the low-loss end, you may have find risks that are quite likely but have relatively small impacts. Even though they are above the threshold curve, you may decide to "self-insure" against these risks, setting aside a kitty of money or schedule time to accommodate them should they occur rather than planning to mitigate them. For example, when traveling on an airline, damage to baggage is a fairly likely risk but one that most travelers accept rather than attempting to mitigate actively.

At the other end of this range you may find some catastrophic risks with unacceptably high total losses, even though their likelihood places them below the threshold line. You may feel more comfortable managing these risks actively, rather than leaving them to chance. This might be compared to buying life insurance for an airline flight. Most people decide against buying

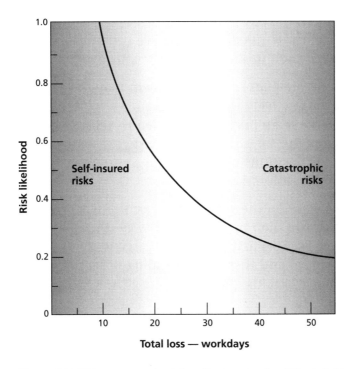

Figure 6-3. Risk map emphasizing the two ends of the total loss spectrum, where you may decide to prioritize risks differently.

such insurance, due to the very low probability of a fatal occurrence, but if it helps you to feel more comfortable on the flight, or if other conditions make this risk particularly significant for you, insurance might be a wise choice.

This is not the last you will read about risk maps. Beyond helping you at this stage to prioritize your risks and decide on an appropriate level of risk management, this graphic is an excellent tool for ongoing monitoring of the project risks currently under active management, as well as those that may come under management later. Risk maps help both the team and management quickly see the risk "picture" for the project and how it is evolving.

3. DEVELOP A PRIORITIZED LIST

Using your risk list—sorted by expected loss—and your risk map, you will need to reach a final consensus with your team on which risks you will manage. Referring to the risk map, the project manager should annotate on the spreadsheet those risks that are above the threshold line as being active. Those below the threshold should be annotated as inactive.

As described in the previous section, the team may have opted not to manage certain risks actively even though they were above the threshold line. Conversely, the team may have decided to actively manage some risks that are below the threshold line. In either case, the spreadsheet needs to reflect the decisions of the team by simply annotating active or inactive in the status column.

Now sort the risk data on the spreadsheet according to risk status (i.e., active or inactive) and then by expected loss value. Table 6-2 illustrates such a prioritized list. Sort first by status in ascending order (to place the active risks at the top) and then in descending order using the expected loss column. You can do this quickly by using the sorting utility in your spreadsheet program.

KEY IDEA

The team will actively manage all risks with active status, while inactive risks will only be monitored. That is, you will simply follow some risks without committing resources actively to diminishing them. By not actively managing all identified risks, you are accepting the fact that you will let some unmanaged risk events occur. But remember, *you are attempting to manage actively the risks that could do the most harm to the project.* Of those risks that have been identified as active, your prioritization also tells you which ones you are going to tackle first. Making such distinctions is exactly the objective of this risk prioritization step.

After you have sorted by status (i.e., whether active or inactive) and expected loss, you need to review the finalized spreadsheet with your team to ensure that consensus has been achieved on which risks are to be managed and the priority ranking. This is accomplished by using the priority column, as seen in Table 6-2, which shows the urgency with which the project's risks will be managed.

Often we are asked, "How many risks should we try to manage?" Unfortunately, the answer to this question depends upon the nature and objectives of your project and on the organization's attitude toward risk. Because you will be committing resources to managing the risks on your active list, you face a balancing act between devoting resources to managing risks versus

Table 6-2. After you sort the risks based upon the expected loss, you should reach consensus with the team on the final priority. Some risks have impacts so high that the team may decide to actively manage them, "overriding" where they fit in rank order.

Priority	Risk Identifier	Status	Probability of Risk Event (P_e)	Probability of Impact (P_i)	Likelihood ($P_e \times P_i$)	Total Loss in Workdays (L_t)	Expected Loss ($P_e \times P_i \times L_t = L_e$)
1	R16	Active	0.9	1	0.9	22	19.8
2	R1	Active	0.7	0.9	0.63	25	15.8
3	R13	Active	0.9	0.9	0.81	17	13.8
4	R5	Active	0.5	0.9	0.45	22	9.9
5	R2	Active	0.7	0.7	0.49	15	7.4
6	R10	Active	0.1	0.5	0.05	25	1.3
7	R4	Inactive	0.7	0.9	0.63	5	3.2
8	R18	Inactive	0.3	0.9	0.27	10	2.7
9	R7	Inactive	0.3	0.7	0.21	13	2.7
10	R9	Inactive	0.3	0.5	0.15	4	0.6

Indicates which risks the team has decided to monitor after reviewing which risks are above the threshold line on the risk map.

simply devoting the same resources to completing the project and taking your chances on the inactive risks. (In Chapter 7, we offer guidance on establishing a rational balance.) Team members must decide how many risks they can manage *effectively*, but as a general rule of thumb we advocate no more than 10 risks to be active at any given time on the priority list. We use the top 10 list as a means to identify those priority risks the team is managing actively. (It may be fewer or more, but the overall number normally should be close to 10.) Chapter 8 outlines some metrics you can use to monitor risk management effectiveness, and the top 10 list can support your risk metrics.

4. COMMUNICATE THE PRIORITIZED LIST

Some people may be concerned that the team will not be managing some known risks. Naturally this can cause discomfort, especially with management. However, to help overcome some of these concerns, you should ensure that everyone connected with the project or managing it understands the product development team's decisions and why certain risks will be managed while others will not. We have found it very useful, after the prioritization efforts are completed, for the project manager to conduct a risk management review to present the results of the team's efforts in selecting their prioritized list.

We suggest that the review involve the managers sponsoring the project, the product development team (which developed the prioritized list), and those individuals who are going to contribute development effort to the project. However, the extent and depth of this review will depend greatly on management's style and availability, so you will have to adapt the list below to fit your circumstances.

We suggest, if you can accomplish it, this rather complete agenda, which will help you gain buy-in to your project's risk management approach:

- team introductions
- risk management process flowchart
- risk activities the team has completed to date
- risk map
- top 10 list (prioritized list that shows risks with active status) stating risk events and impacts along with expected loss

- review of the risk data (drivers, probabilities, total and expected loss) for each risk on the top 10 list
- "inactive" risks stating risk events and impacts along with expected loss
- next steps (which will be to develop risk resolution activities for the top 10 list)

During this review, if your management team has not been trained in formal risk management, expect to receive many questions—and even challenges—on terms, the process, and your risk data. When we introduce risk management into organizations, one of our first activities is training the management team on the process. We do this to assure that the review sessions stay focused on the risks that are going to be managed by the team and do not become training sessions for people unfamiliar with the techniques. (See Chapter 11 for more information.)

CAUTION

Running Example

This hypothetical example is meant only to illustrate the risk management techniques described in this book. We do not intend that anyone use this example as a medical reference or modify any personal behavior based on this data.

EXAMPLE

When we left Bernardo at the end of the last chapter, he had analyzed his heart attack risk thoroughly and filled in all parts of the risk model for it. In the meantime he has once again watched the television news intently and is now also concerned about two other risks. In addition to a heart attack that Bernardo believes he might suffer during the next five years, he is also concerned about contracting melanoma within five years (risk event), resulting in his death and loss of salary (impact); and having osteoporosis by age 65 (risk event), resulting in a broken hip, which would prevent him from working for up to one year (impact).

Melanoma is a potentially fatal form of skin cancer. In completing his risk analysis for this disease, Bernardo determines that he is at a small but significant level of risk for this condition because he is fair-skinned, has some family history of skin cancer, and spent his youth under the sun in the Philippines.

Next, Bernardo analyzes his risk for osteoporosis, a condition that decreases bone mass as we age. His analysis reveals that this condition is much more prevalent in older women. Because Bernardo is a 50-year-old male, this fact becomes a risk event driver (drivers can also *decrease* the probability or indicate a *low* probability). Therefore, he believes the probability for this risk event is low due to the driver (other drivers must be evaluated to make a full determination of the health risks).

Table 6-3 presents the risk data as a result of completing Bernardo's prioritization. He has decided that he is going to actively manage the heart attack but not manage the identified risks of melanoma and osteoporosis. He made these decisions based upon results from his risk analysis and prioritization.

Table 6-3. Bernardo's prioritized health risks based on results from his risk analysis.

Risk identifier	Status	Probability of risk event (P_e)	Probability of impact (P_i)	Likelihood $(P_e \times P_i)$	Total loss in workdays (L_t)	Expected loss $(P_e \times P_i \times L_t = L_e)$
1. Heart attack	Active	0.5	0.7	0.35	US$1,500,000	US$525,000
2. Melanoma	Inactive	0.1	0.5	0.05	US$1,500,000	US$75,000
3. Osteoporosis	Inactive	0.1	0.1	0.01	US$50,000	US$500

Summary

Risk prioritization allows the team to focus on those risks most likely to keep the project from meeting its stated goals while not devoting undue resources to lesser risks. By using the quantified risk data, the team can decide which risks are worthy of their active attention and which risks they will only monitor. In the next chapter, the team will make further decisions on what type of action to take on the risks marked for active attention.

Supplementary Reading

A Guide to the Project Management Body of Knowledge. Newtown Square, Pennsylvania: Project Management Institute, 2000. Instead of portraying risks on a map, some people prefer to use a matrix with the same axes. See Figure 11-3 for an example of such a matrix.

MIL-STD 882D, *System Safety Program Requirements.* Washington, DC: United States Department of Defense. February 10, 2000. This military standard addresses hazards in the product itself rather than project risks, but it uses a related approach for prioritizing "mishap risks" (see Table A-III).

7
STEP 4—PLANNING RESOLUTION OF TARGETED RISKS

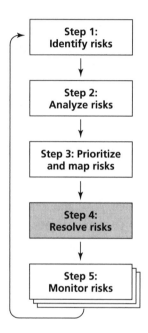

At this point in the risk management process you should have a short list of your most critical risks, obtained by using the process described in the previous chapter. Now you will formulate action plans for dealing with each active risk identified on the top 10 list. Finally, in the next chapter, "Step 5—Monitoring Project Risks," you will periodically reassess all risks and consider whether inactive risks should become active or whether active risks can be closed as you mitigate them. Consequently, this short list is dynamic and will change as you progress through the project.

This step's goal is to develop risk action plans to reduce the probability of the risk event and lessen its damage if it does occur. The most important concept in this chapter is that action plans are designed to change the risk

KEY IDEA

drivers to the point that they no longer drive the likelihood of the risks. This might sound counterintuitive, but effective risk management does not engage the *risk* itself; it instead seeks to change the *risk drivers* (that is, its underlying facts). If the risk drivers are eradicated, then the risk has been eliminated.

CAUTION

These plans then become tasks within the overall product development project. They are treated with the same importance as any other project tasks, as you will see as we move into the final step in the next chapter. We pointed out in Chapter 1 that a common failing of project risk management is that such action plans, though developed, are not taken seriously and so are never carried out. Consequently, remain mindful as you develop your plans that they are indeed actionable!

The hard work that goes into risk management will be wasted if you don't work aggressively to reduce the likelihood of risk occurrence and the magnitude of the total loss. The actions you take on your top 10 list of risks must be cost effective, action-oriented, and—above all else—followed through with precision in order to sustain an effective risk management program. All the work done up to this point is aimed at creating action plans that change the project landscape to minimize disruption to the project's goals.

Risk Resolution Process

In resolving risks, you have various options, as suggested by Figure 7-1. We present most of these options in the next section to expand your thinking about how you can resolve a risk. At the top level of Figure 7-1, you would normally proceed to consider action plans, but you may find that you lack the information to take action now. This should not be an excuse for not taking action, so if you choose it, assign it with a definite objective, due date, staffing, and resources. Alternatively, you may believe that the needed information will become available at a certain date, so you can set a date for re-evaluation without resources or staffing in the interim. Finally, you may decide to do nothing about the risk; that is, you accept the consequences of the risks when they occur, as you have already decided for risks on your inactive list.

Similar to designing a product, deciding which actions to take is often a cyclic process for each risk. You formulate plans and compare them based

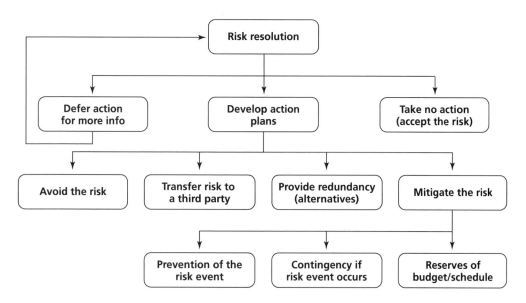

Figure 7-1. Risk resolution planning process for each risk, showing options available at three different levels.

on effectiveness, risk reduction leverage, implementation time, political expediency, or another criterion. If the results are unacceptable, you must go back and refine your information, then try again until you have an action plan that is adequate, cost-effective, and reliable.

You may also find that your solution approach can be applied incrementally. For example, you can do various amounts of software testing to identify and eliminate bugs, or you can purchase multiple workstations so that engineers needn't wait excessively to use them. Many such variable solutions exhibit the phenomenon of diminishing returns, so you may have to test varying degrees of the solution to arrive at the most cost-effective variation.

As you create your action plans, you may find the tools and approaches in Chapters 9 and 10 to be helpful. Some of these tools, such as risk simulation and decision analysis, can be time-consuming to apply. You will have to decide, based on the impact of the risk you are considering, how much effort you should put into analyzing it and planning for its resolution. Any labor you put into resolving the risk is part of its ultimate cost, so keep an eye on the potential benefits as you run up the costs.

CAUTION

Normally, the outcome (deliverable) from this process is an action plan, or plans—perhaps one prevention plan and one contingency plan per risk. But the number and type of plans you develop depends on the existence of feasible plans and their effectiveness. If the prevention plan reduces the impact to a tolerable level, or you find that your contingency plan's marginal benefit does not justify its cost, you may decide to accept the residual expected loss due to the contingency plan.

KEY IDEA

You might not even find action plans whose benefits exceed their cost. In this case, you may have to accept the risk; that is, accept the do-nothing option. If you accept a risk and forego an action plan, you should establish a *reserve*, a kitty of money or a buffer of schedule slack equal to the residual expected loss.

This contingency reserve keeps you honest about your project's risk. If the combined contingency reserve is small (for all risks on your top 10 list), it is not too important; but if it is large, it might cause you to rethink the whole project or even cancel it.

Action Planning

You will be developing action plans for each active risk on your top 10 list. Typically, the project manager and team will assign a risk owner for each risk. This individual will take charge of developing appropriate action plans. Risk owners may select a subteam to assist in developing a set of action plans. After being assigned a risk, the risk owner and his or her subteam typically can take four different actions to manage their risk:

- Avoid the risk by reversing the decisions that were made that caused the risk to arise in the first place.
- Transfer the risk to another entity.
- Provide redundant paths to increase the likelihood of success.
- Mitigate the risk by developing prevention and contingency plans along with adequate reserves of time and money for risks you accept, risks not fully mitigated, and some protection for unknown risks that may occur.

Your course of action will normally become clear as you evaluate drivers of the risk event and the impact. Figure 7-2 shows how the Standard Risk Model suggests multiple planning approaches and how the different actions affect the components of the model. Transfer and redundancy actions typically act on the risk events (sometimes they can be applied to the drivers). As you will see below, avoidance and prevention plans normally affect the risk event drivers, and contingency plans and reserves generally aim at the impact drivers. These differences are critical—they guide you to where to look to manage risks.

KEY IDEA

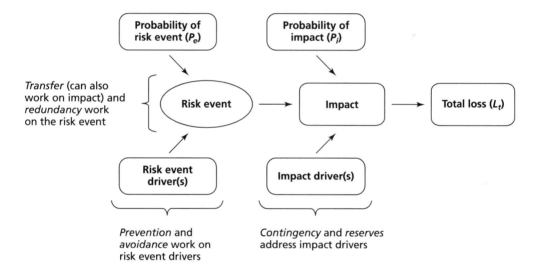

Figure 7-2. The Standard Risk Model showing how action plans are targeted at different elements of the model.

If your workshops have been successful, you should be able to determine fairly quickly the best action to follow. After your action plans have been developed, you should document the targeted action plans. We recommend you continue to use the risk tracking spreadsheet that you started in Chapter 4 to document your plans. Look ahead to Figure 8-2 for a good example of documenting a risk along with its action plans.

The risk owner then has the responsibility to bring the results of the action planning to the project team to present the preferred paths. Once again, the team should strive to achieve group consensus on the actions, particularly if the action plan is costly or significant amounts of effort are needed to support the action plan.

The following sections describe various actions you can take against risks you have placed on your top 10 list. Remember, you are only going to spend time and energy on those risks the team has decided to manage actively.

AVOIDANCE

Risk exists on a project because you make decisions, implicitly or explicitly. The results of those decisions become risk event drivers that affect the likelihood that risk events will occur. For example, the needs of the business might encourage you to make decisions to introduce a product into the marketplace prematurely, or even start full production on a new manufacturing line before the manufacturing process has been fully validated. However, often you can simply avoid the risk by reversing the original decisions that led you into this situation.

We continually work with teams that introduce unnecessary risks. By "unnecessary," we mean risks that do not offer a potential benefit. If you are going to introduce risk into your project, there must be a clear potential for an offsetting advantage.

EXAMPLE For example, we worked with a software development team that decided to switch to a new operating system for their application software. During the risk identification and analysis workshops, several risks surfaced regarding the new operating system. We asked the team why they wanted to switch to the new operating system. Their response: "The product performance is greatly improved." At first glance, this reasoning seemed absolutely correct; however, when we probed a little further, we determined that customers had no intention of switching operating systems—even when the performance improvements were presented to them. The customer's reasoning was that the cost of upgrading to the new operating system was more expensive than the cost savings that could be realized with the performance improvements in the product. In the end, the switch to the new operating system was not made, and many risks were eliminated by way of simple avoidance.

When electing to use this course of action, be careful not to become risk averse. We are not advocating that risks be avoided altogether, for innovation cannot occur without taking on risks. However, you need to know your limits on how much risk your projects can tolerate. In addition, the team needs to be cognizant of its limitations, particularly regarding the introduction of new technology on a project.

CAUTION

See Chapter 10 for other ways in which you can avoid risk and for a more systemic viewpoint on risk avoidance.

TRANSFER

A team often considers a transfer action plan when it recognizes that it lacks the expertise to introduce a certain new technology in a new product. To maintain the desired schedule for product launch, they may decide to *transfer* the risk to another entity, such as a contractor who has experience in developing this type of technology. The primary motivator for making a transfer decision is to protect the project's timeline.

Let us explore an example of how this would be used. Assume that the marketing group has determined that a particular feature will become a critical customer requirement when the market window for it opens in about six months. However, the engineering group's feasibility study may have revealed that the technology needed to introduce the feature is not an engineering competency now, and it would take about a year to develop the feature, including the learning delay. The study has also shown that a particular contractor already has a solution that could be integrated into the current product in about six months.

EXAMPLE

The absence of expertise in this technology now becomes a risk event driver to a risk event such as, "Introduction of XYZ technology will take longer than six months to develop." The team may decide that the best course of action is to contract out the feature to the experienced third party. It is important to note that by contracting out the feature, the risk did *not* disappear—you only *transferred* the risk to someone who you believe has a greater potential to complete the feature development in the six-month timeframe. It is now up to the contractor to actively manage the risk because new technology is still being introduced.

Market risk is another area where a transfer plan could be used. Perhaps the associated market risk event is, "The market will not be ready for XYZ technology when we introduce it in six months." In this case, you might transfer the risk by engaging an advertising or public relations firm to prepare the market for your new technology.

KEY IDEA

A final point: when you transfer a risk, you are usually only transferring the *risk event*, not the impact. Even though in the initial example we subcontracted out a feature with new technology to an experienced contractor, if the contractor does not meet your delivery needs, it is *your* bottom line that is going to be impacted. In this example, you would need to be involved with the contractor's risk management activities just as though you were doing the development.

REDUNDANCY

Many product development teams use this technique without realizing it. Redundancy comes into play when you employ parallel solution paths to improve your chances that an effective solution will emerge. You can think of redundancy as being akin to having a backup system if the primary system fails. Redundancy addresses the risk event, or even the impact, but it typically does not act on the drivers of either. For instance, if a team is concerned that a new custom part will not meet specifications (risk event), they may decide to have two suppliers develop the part (redundancy plan). This action plan did nothing to change the risk event drivers of why you originally believed the custom part would not meet "specs" in the first place.

EXAMPLE Consider an example of applying redundancy effectively. MDS Sciex, a Canadian manufacturer of analytical instruments, used an interesting double application of redundancy on a mass spectrometer development project. They wanted to use an integrated version of a split-flow turbo molecular pump to gain additional pump capacity and reduce product cost. An integrated pump performs better due to improved vacuum conductance, and it is less expensive because it does not need its own housing. Unfortunately, an integrated pump results in the technical risk of a highly coupled system between the turbo pumps and the mass spectrometer's vacuum chamber. It also carries the business risk of being locked into a single turbo pump supplier. Consequently, the team's first redundancy plan was to design an alternative vacuum chamber using discrete (not integrated) pumps. Their second redundancy plan involved developing another turbo pump supplier for integrated turbo pump technology so that they would have a second source.

In product development, a common application is to start two separate development efforts to engineer a solution. This is particularly useful when dealing with two unproven and competing technologies, or if you are unsure which of two product attributes your customers will prefer. If you develop two solutions, you increase the likelihood that one of them will succeed. Clearly, the downside is the cost of conducting two development efforts. This action has also been called the "shotgun approach," so exercise it only when your due diligence reveals that the benefits outweigh the cost. However, if you have a solid understanding of your cost of delay, you may find that the cost of the development is small compared to the project delay if the single development effort failed. This type of action depends strongly on the amount of "insurance" the project wants to purchase.

You can also combine transfer and redundancy plans. For example, when developing their API 2000 mass spectrometer, MDS Sciex found that they lacked the expertise they needed in turbo molecular pumping, specifically in a new split-flow technology. Thus, they used competitive bidding to select two (redundancy) contractors (transfer). Each contractor demonstrated a working prototype of a split-flow turbo molecular pump operating in MDS Sciex's mass spectrometer breadboard. The successful candidate, based on this performance testing, was used in the final product.

EXAMPLE

More examples of redundancy appear in Chapter 10 (see the section entitled "Stay Flexible on Unresolved Issues").

MITIGATION

To mitigate means to make something less severe. Mitigation plans are probably the most powerful type of action plan you can develop. Observe that transfer simply shifts responsibility for the risk—often only partially—to someone else; and redundancy just dilutes the risk. Mitigation, in contrast, targets root causes. You will be able to develop plans for prevention of the risk event and in case the risk event still occurs, you can

KEY IDEA

develop contingency plans to cope with the impact. Due to the importance of risk mitigation, we treat it and its components, prevention and contingency, in separate sections.

Mitigation Actions

Mitigation is the mainstay of effective risk management. In this section, we first describe some attributes of risk mitigation common to prevention and contingency plans. Then we describe each type of plan and the attributes that differentiate them.

EXAMPLE

Mitigation actions are designed to counter the effects of risk event and impact drivers directly. For instance, if a risk event driver is stated as "customer has not approved the requirements," it is common sense to develop a prevention plan to change the risk event driver. You would simply have the customer review and approve the requirements. Once the customer has approved the requirements, the risk event driver becomes "customer has approved the requirements," which now diminishes the probability of the risk event. Notice in this example that we did not even mention the risk event; we only described the risk event driver, which illustrates the point that mitigation actions do not pursue the risk events and impacts but instead their drivers.

KEY IDEA

We have found that if project teams have generated high-quality risk event and impact drivers, the mitigation action often becomes obvious. Conversely, we have also observed that when a team struggles to develop mitigation actions, it is usually due to weak driver descriptions. We have also seen good mitigation actions that do not map back to a risk event or impact driver, which usually means that an important driver was not listed originally.

When developing mitigation actions, verify that you meet the following criteria:

- Make actions specific.
- Define trigger points that start preparations and actions.
- Estimate the time and resources required to support actions.
- Estimate how much the probability estimates for the risk event and impact will decrease if the plans are successful.

- Assess cost effectiveness by using the risk reduction leverage formula as described in the section, "Balancing Benefits with Cost," later in this chapter.
- Assign an owner to implement the plan.
- Decide how you will monitor the plan. (How will you know whether it is achieving its objective?)

The "trigger points" you define for mitigation actions are key. Trigger points can be dates, project milestones, or conditions. You can think of a trigger point as a starter's gun in a race. It signifies to everyone that an action is about to commence. When used with a mitigation plan, trigger points can be incorporated into the schedule if you are triggering from a date, time period, or milestone. Conditions come into play when you define some type of threshold to trigger actions for your plans. For instance, you may decide a contingency plan will use developers as an additional resource in helping to create system requirements. If you do, you need to know when you should engage the assistance of the developers. One team, for example, had a similar contingency plan and they simply monitored the output of the systems engineering group. When their output dropped below seven requirements per day, the team engaged the developers to assist with this task.

KEY IDEA

EXAMPLE

Also keep in mind that risk management is not free. There is a cost (in time and money) associated with each mitigation action. You must integrate mitigation action tasks into the schedule or your team will not take them seriously! In addition, your project budget must take into account the cost of implementing these plans. Nothing is gained—and, in fact, you are weakening your credibility—if your mitigation actions are not adequately funded. You may have to reset schedules and budgets to reflect your risk management efforts, even to the point of terminating the project if the cost or schedule impact of mitigation undercut the project's viability.

KEY IDEA

PREVENTION PLANNING

The first type of mitigation action to explore is the prevention plan. Figure 7-3 shows how a prevention plan acts on risk event drivers. Notice that after plan implementation, the risk event driver changes and the probability estimate for the risk event decreases. By decreasing the probability of the risk event, you decrease the expected loss of the entire risk. This is how you can determine if your prevention plans are effective. Conversely, you might find that the probability is not decreasing, indicating that the prevention plan is not as effective as envisioned. This is why it is important to have multiple plans to address various drivers.

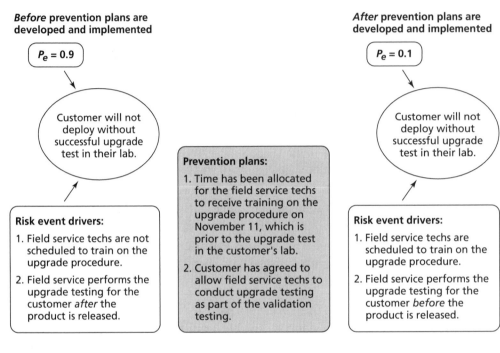

Figure 7-3. The risk event portion of the Standard Risk Model illustrates how prevention plans can change the risk event drivers, thereby reducing the probability of the risk event from occurring.

Risk owners should work with a subteam (if assigned) to evaluate each risk event driver and determine what possible actions could be implemented to counter each driver. Don't worry if you cannot develop a plan for every driver. Even if you cannot simply alter the project environment to minimize the probability of the risk event occurring, you can still develop plans that help minimize the effect of the driver. For instance, you might be concerned about the risk of your car breaking down on a long trip because of the risk event driver that the car is 25 years old. Since you cannot change the age of the car (short of buying a newer one), you must develop prevention plans to fully inspect and repair (if needed) the components that tend to fail more often on older cars. Even though you did not change the risk event driver, you did minimize the effects of age on the car.

When your team uses a spreadsheet to track its progress in risk management, you will find it useful to connect each risk event driver to one or more prevention plans. This helps the team determine which plans are effective (Figure 8-2 will illustrate such a spreadsheet).

CONTINGENCY PLANNING

Contingency planning is the second type of mitigation action. Figure 7-4 shows how a contingency plan acts on an impact driver to reduce the probability of the impact. Normally, we prefer to reduce the probability of the impact rather than reduce the total loss. This allows us to monitor the summation of total loss along with the summation of the expected loss for

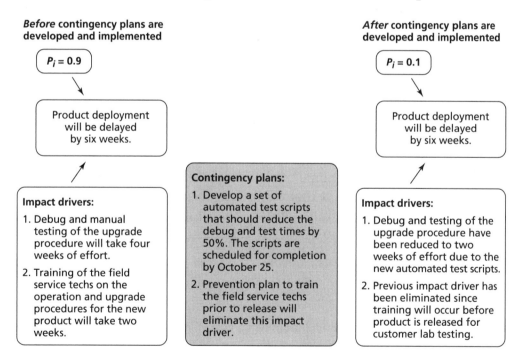

Figure 7-4. The impact portion of the Standard Risk Model illustrates how contingency plans can change the impact drivers, thereby reducing the probability of the impact from occurring.

113

all risks on the top 10 list as a measure of risk management effectiveness. (Chapter 8 covers risk management metrics in more depth.) However, accuracy should prevail over monitoring convenience, so if you can reflect the improvement more accurately by changing total loss, do so.

CAUTION

Although you invoke contingency plans after the risk event occurs, many teams fail to recognize that contingency planning must be done beforehand. For instance, assume that a supplier is considering discontinuing a particular type of microprocessor your team has been using. If the risk event occurs (that is, the microprocessor is discontinued before adequate quantities of your product can be produced), the impact will be six months of lost revenue. You may have a plan to switch to a new microprocessor, but it will take six months to complete. However, you decide to train a small group of software developers to use the tool set for the new microprocessor and to develop some prototype software for it, which reduces the switch time from six months to three. You must complete all of this preparation before the old microprocessor is discontinued (the risk event).

RESERVES

Product development teams cannot identify every risk that arises on a project. These types of risks are considered "unknown." Some people call them "unknown unknown" risks, meaning that not only is their magnitude unknown, but so is their very existence. Often, teams develop reserves or buffers of time, money, or some other loss quantity to account for them. The problem with reserves is that teams mistakenly rely on them to fully cover all the risks they identified in the workshops. We advise that you use reserves only for covering losses in the following conditions:

- Unknown risks that may occur.
- Impacts that still occur despite contingency plans that may have been put in place.
- Inactive risks the team identified at the workshop but decided to accept.

Setting the level of reserves is difficult at best. However, we offer the following tips to help set up appropriate reserve levels to compensate for unknown risks. First off, history is your best ally. Review any past project documentation for events that triggered losses. Determine if any of those events could possibly be experienced by your project, and develop a reserve that could have compensated for them. For the reserves provided against incomplete contingency plans and inactive risks, the size of these reserves will depend on the quality of your contingency plans and how well you selected the most harmful risks to manage. Your calculated expected losses for these risks should help you size your reserves against them.

Admittedly, trying to develop a reserve to compensate for unknowns is very challenging. Some organizations we have worked with simply used a policy-based schedule reserve of 5 to 10 percent of the overall project duration as a time buffer, even when using the risk management process described in this book. The critical point is that you not rely on reserves as your sole contingency—slipping schedules and budgets are the antithesis of risk management.

CAUTION

Balancing Benefits with Cost

As you proceed to action planning, you will start making commitments to expend resources—financial or human—to prevent a risk or to deal with it if it occurs. Although you might have had some concern about the cost of risk management all along, at this point you should analyze explicitly how the cost of implementing and executing prevention and contingency plans compares with the benefits received.

A couple of situations will demonstrate how you can compare costs with benefits. The first example is the risk of being blocked in your driveway next winter by a blizzard.

EXAMPLE

The impact is that you arrive at work late, and you can put a cost on this (angry boss, getting fired, etc.). The benefit side of your calculation is reducing or eliminating this impact. One option for a plan is to buy a snow thrower, which you can amortize over several years. This is a contingency plan, because the possibility of being blocked in by the blizzard still exists. But this can be your lowest-cost option, and it could reduce the impact (how late you arrive at work) to acceptable levels. In short, it could provide the greatest benefit for the cost incurred. You could contract with a snowplowing service to eliminate the blockage before you arise, which is a prevention plan because you will never know your driveway was blocked. You could move to a residence without a driveway, which is a prevention plan whose cost can be more difficult to calculate. Lastly, you could do nothing—that is, accept the risk—if the cost of any of these options exceeds the benefit derived. But you opt for the do-nothing option only *after* completing the calculations, not because you ignored or denied the risk.

EⓍAMPLE That example was unfair to those who live in California and cannot imagine a blizzard. So, for them, we consider an earthquake whose impact is that it topples your house. The most obvious solution here is the contingency plan of buying earthquake insurance. But such insurance can be very high in cost and of limited benefit (due to high deductibles), or even unobtainable. A more proactive contingency plan is to bolt your sill plate to the foundation more securely and install so-called hurricane straps, which will provide limited benefit at reasonable cost, and it could also make earthquake insurance obtainable or affordable, providing another contingency plan. Consequently, from a cost-benefit perspective, this could be your "best buy." You could avoid the risk entirely (prevention) by moving to Vermont, trading earthquakes for blizzards, but the cost (change in lifestyle) of this option would exceed the benefit for most Californians. Notice that the potential loss is catastrophic in this case, so a do-nothing option (accepting the risk) will probably not stand up under analysis.

Observe some characteristics of these candidate action plans:

- Except for the do-nothing option, each plan has both a cost and a benefit associated with it.
- The cost can exceed the benefit, in which case the plan is unwise.
- Often, the plan provides only a partial, but perhaps adequate, benefit.
- Usually, the best action plan is the one with the highest benefit-to-cost ratio.
- Even if you have a good prevention plan, unless it is perfect, you will usually also need a contingency plan.

All but the last of these points are summarized in the following formula for *risk reduction leverage* of an action plan:

$$Risk\ reduction\ leverage\ =\ \frac{Expected\ loss_{before} - Expected\ loss_{after}}{Cost}$$

where *before* and *after* are relative to implementing and executing your plan, and *Cost* is the cost of doing so. You use this formula to calculate the leverage of each candidate action plan. Unless there are extenuating circumstances, you then choose the plan with the greatest leverage. However, if no candidate has a leverage above 1.0, you either choose the do-nothing option or keep searching until you find a plan whose benefits exceed its costs of implementation and execution.

Usually, the cost of implementing and executing your action plan (the denominator in the formula above) will appear in monetary terms, but the benefit (numerator) is likely to be in expressed in time units (schedule delay). To proceed, you must either convert time to monetary units or vice versa. (The "Supplementary Reading" lists a source for making this conversion, based on the economics of your project.) The conversion factor, which we call the cost of delay, can range from less than a thousand dollars per day to over a million dollars per day, so it is important that you complete this calculation for your project. Without it, you will not know whether the action plan you are contemplating is excellent or foolhardy.

SCOPE

CAUTION

Running Example

Here we continue the example of Bernardo, a 50-year-old male who is concerned about having a heart attack. This hypothetical example is meant only to illustrate the risk management techniques described in this book. As previously stated, we do not intend that anyone use this example as a medical reference or modify any personal behavior based on this data.

EXAMPLE

When we left Bernardo at the end of the last chapter, he had decided that he was going to manage his heart attack risk actively and let the other two risks remain inactive. He knows that his action plans should stem from his risk event and impact drivers, so he first reviews the risk event drivers and determines what he can do to resolve the risk. Refer to Table 7-1 to see how he connected the risk event drivers to each prevention plan he developed. Notice that he accepts the fact he is a 50-year-old male and determines there is nothing he can do about this particular risk event driver. However,

Table 7-1. Connecting risk event drivers to prevention plans for a heart attack risk.

Risk Event Drivers	Prevention Plans	Implementation?
1. Stressful job.	1. Take stress management courses starting on June 13.	Yes
	2. Request to be re-assigned to a different job function.	Yes
2. 50-year-old male.	1. None.	N/A
3. No regular exercise.	1. Schedule appointment for June 3 with doctor for health evaluation and to develop a safe exercise program.	Yes
	2. Starting on June 10 an exercise program will be initiated.	Yes
4. Excessively overweight.	1. Schedule appointment for June 3 with doctor for health evaluation and to develop a safe diet program.	Yes
	2. Starting on June 10 a doctor-supervised diet will be started.	Yes
5. High blood pressure.	Covered by stress relief plans above.	—

Table 7-2. Connecting impact drivers to contingency plans for a heart attack risk.

Impact Drivers	Contingency Plans	Implementation?
1. 50 miles from the ambulance.	1. Work with village trustees to acquire an ambulance service. Next meeting is scheduled for June 17.	Yes
	2. Place house for sale on June 3 and move closer to a larger city.	No
2. 100 miles to the nearest hospital.	1. Work with village trustees to acquire an immediate care facility. Next meeting is scheduled for June 17.	Yes
	2. Place house for sale on June 3 and move closer to a larger city.	No
3. Spouse does not drive.	1. Schedule driving lessons for spouse. Current cost estimates are US$25 an hour but the closest place offering driving lessons is 50 miles from the village.	No
	2. Starting on June 4, I will provide driving lessons for my spouse. We are targeting to complete the lessons by July 9. We have an appointment scheduled for July 16 for the driving exam.	Yes
4. Will make US$100,000 per year until retirement at age 65.	1. Take out life insurance policy equal to the value of the expected loss.	Yes

the other risk event drivers allow prevention plans, so ultimately he can change those drivers into less harmful facts.

Next, Bernardo reviews the impact drivers and develops contingency plans in the event he does have a heart attack, which still could occur even though he has developed a prevention strategy that has reduced the risk event. Table 7-2 illustrates how he connects each impact driver to a contingency plan. Note that most of his contingency plans require preparations; for instance, if he convinces his spouse to learn to drive or to move closer to the hospital, obviously he will need to do this *before* he has the heart attack.

Finally, he decides on the prevention and contingency plans that he will implement. Also, Bernardo re-estimates the probabilities for the risk event and impact assuming that the mitigation plans he has selected will be successful, and then he develops an estimate of the cost to implement his prevention and contingency plans. He then uses the risk reduction leverage formula to ensure that his mitigation plans are cost-effective. Table 7-3 outlines the expected losses before and after his mitigation efforts. As you

Table 7-3. Expected loss calculations based upon projected outcomes of the prevention and contingency plans for a heart attack risk.

	Before Action Plans	After Action Plans	Notes
Probability of Risk Event (P_e)	0.5	0.1	Significant strides can be made in lowering the probability of suffering from a heart attack by implementing the stated prevention plans.
Probability of Impact (P_i)	0.7	0.3	Bernardo has decided not to implement the most effective contingencies (moving closer to medical facilities) since all of his family lives in his current village. In addition, working to acquire an ambulance service and an immediate care facility will not be completed in the short term
Total Loss (L_t)	US$1,500,000	US$1,500,000	This value represents the loss of salary in the event that Bernardo dies at age 50. We developed the loss value from the impact drivers of losing $100,000 of salary per year over a 15-year period, none of which can be improved easily.
Expected Loss (L_e)	US$525,000	US$45,000	Current estimates show that a significant reduction in risk can be achieved with mitigation plans. In this example, we are not applying the results of a payout from a life insurance policy that would also decrease the expected loss value.

can see from the table, Bernardo has reduced his expected loss from US$525,000 to US$45,000, mainly by implementing his prevention plans.

Summary

In this chapter, we described the process for resolving project risks effectively. You should first decide on the risk resolution path: are you going to delay action and research for more information, decide to take action, or simply accept the risk and do nothing? For risks *not* on the top 10 list, you accept them and do nothing, by definition.

If you decide to take action, you should focus on the risk event and impact drivers so you can diminish the likelihood of your risks. The four actions of avoidance, transfer, redundancy, and mitigation are the primary options available to actively manage those risks you have identified on your top 10 list.

In Chapter 8, you will see how action plans are monitored.

Supplementary Reading

Boehm, Barry W. *Software Risk Management*. Washington, DC: IEEE Computer Society Press, 1989. Provides numerical examples illustrating use of the risk reduction leverage formula, including comparison of alternative plans (page 8).

Conrow, Edmund H. Risk management. Chapter 17 in Kerzner, Harold, *Project Management*, Seventh Edition. New York: John Wiley, 2001. Offers additional methods for generating mitigation plans, or what the author calls "risk control actions" (page 935).

Smith, Preston G. and Reinertsen, Donald G. *Developing Products in Half the Time*. New York: John Wiley & Sons, 1998. Chapter 2 of this book is devoted to describing how to calculate the six trade-offs between schedule slip, project budget overrun, product target cost overrun, and product performance shortfalls for your project. This will help you express, say, project expense items in project delay terms so that you can compare and prioritize risks. It will also allow you to compare the cost of an action plan (often expressed in monetary terms) with the benefit offered by this plan (usually in time schedule delay terms).

8
STEP 5—MONITORING PROJECT RISKS

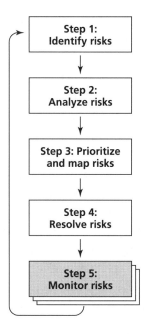

As the diagram above suggested, this last step of the risk management process differs from preceding ones. Whereas you generally conduct the other steps once per project, this one is an ongoing activity to ensure that your action plans are making progress, that successful plans are retired, and that any significant new or growing risks are taken under management. This is where the payoff from risk management occurs, but it occurs only if you are vigilant in monitoring your program. We observed in Chapter 1 that some organizations do well up to this point, but then fail to follow through—much to their embarrassment when their well-analyzed risks start materializing because they had not followed their action plans.

During the prioritizing and risk-mapping step, we introduced the concept of risk status by declaring each risk in your tracking spreadsheet to be either active or inactive depending on your final prioritization decisions. As you enter the monitoring phase of risk management, you will add two additional types of risk status: issue and closed.

Change the risk status to "issue" when a risk event labeled active occurs despite prevention plans that may have been in place. In the ideal setting, prevention plans would reduce the probability of risk events to zero. However, in reality, some identified risk events will still occur; they then become issues to manage. We consider "issue management" to be the implementation of contingency plans to mitigate the total loss. Be sure to track the risk events that became issues so that you can learn which driver ultimately caused the risk event to occur. You can use this information during risk identification workshops for future projects.

The final risk status you can assign to a prioritized risk is "closed." To close a risk, it must meet one of the following criteria:

- The risk event was successfully prevented from occurring.
- The time component (or condition) of the risk event has passed and it did not occur. (Remember that you are dealing with probabilities, so the risk may never materialize, even if you do nothing.)
- The risk event occurred (it has become an issue), and you have completed managing the issue via a contingency plan.

Ongoing Risk Management

Back in Chapter 4, you started a spreadsheet to track your risks through the process, and as you progressed through subsequent chapters you added additional information to it. Figure 8-1 is a breakdown of a how a typical risk-tracking spreadsheet is organized. Notice that, in addition to two summary worksheets for the project, this tracking spreadsheet has one worksheet for each risk. Figure 8-2 illustrates one of these single-risk worksheets.

This figure is only an example. You should experiment with tracking methods that work best for your company's culture. We also recommend that the project manager retain ownership of the spreadsheet in order to maintain continuity in data being entered. Using a spreadsheet is an economical way to monitor your risk progress; however, on projects where

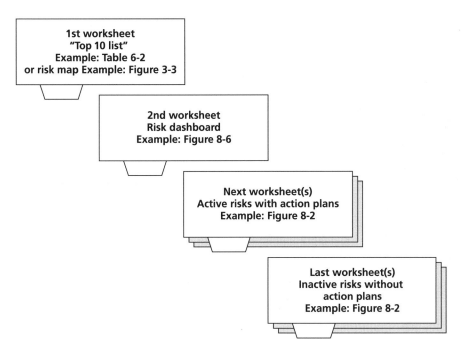

Figure 8-1. Example of how a risk-tracking spreadsheet can be organized to support the risk management process detailed in Chapters 4–8.

many people are making risk updates—especially if they are in different locations or organizations—we have found that it can become cumbersome. To that end, some teams shift from spreadsheets to commercially available tools. Another alternative is a web-based tool following the process outlined in this book, which greatly simplifies data collection and the accessibility of risk management information for all team members. In any case, start with a spreadsheet as a pilot until you determine what you would prefer to have in another medium.

As you reach this step in the risk management process, this spreadsheet should be "finalized" in a form that makes it easy for you to watch the risks that are not under management (i.e., do not have action plans). You can then question regularly whether any of them should come into active management due to changes in the project environment. You also have an action plan for each risk that is under active management. These plans should be integrated into your project monitoring system, just like design tasks or product testing tasks.

Risk Identifier	Priority	Risk Owner	Date Opened	Date Closed	Risk Status	Actual Loss	
R3	1	Lisa Tirem	Sept. 30	Nov. 25	Closed	0	

Risk Event	Impact
RF emissions compliance with FCC standards will not be granted on the first test cycle and will result in the motherboard being reworked.	Field trial with customer will be delayed by six weeks (30 workdays).

Monitor Dates	P_e	P_i	Workdays L_t	Workdays L_e
Sept. 30	0.5	0.9	30	13.5
Oct. 14	0.3	0.9	30	8.1
Oct. 28	0.3	0.9	30	8.1
Nov. 11	0.1	0.5	30	1.5
Nov. 25	0.0	0.3	30	0.0

Risk Event Drivers	Prevention Plans	Impact Drivers	Contingency Plans
1. Previous projects have only achieved a 50 percent first pass success for FCC compliance testing.	1. Early prototypes will be submitted to FCC testing to gain visibility into problem areas. Status: Preliminary testing was completed on early prototypes resulting in two modifications to the motherboard. The modified units have now passed the official FCC testing. This risk is closed.	1. FCC tests will need to be re-run for a second attempt, which takes one week.	1. We will engage a contractor who performs the FCC testing and determine if we can expedite the test process. Status: Contractor has informed us they do not expedite this testing.
2. RF section of the motherboard layout has changed significantly.	2. Extra review time will be allocated on RF sections of the motherboard. Status: Two extra days were spent on the review of the RF section.	2. Correcting and manufacturing new motherboards will take five weeks.	2. Instead of manufacturing new boards overseas, we will use a local manufacturer, which should reduce the time by two weeks. Status: Local manufacturer was used for prototypes, which helped on prevention plan 1.
3. Engineering team has limited design experience in RF emissions reduction.	3. Training will be provided to team on techniques for controlling RF emissions. Status: Team received training on Oct. 7.		

Figure 8-2. This is an example of a spreadsheet being used to track a particular risk. Many companies use the risk data shown here to develop web-based applications to achieve the same result.

PROGRESS ON RESOLUTION

Each action plan must be monitored regularly to ensure that it is progressing toward resolving its risk. If it is a contingency plan, then—just like a fire extinguisher—its monitoring should ensure that it is ready to be implemented should the risk occur before its prevention plan reaches maturity. Also, you should have a means of monitoring any risks for which action has been deferred pending more information.

You can monitor your action plans on two levels. The first is a report on the activity and status of each action plan, the second is an overall map of your progress on all action plans. Monitoring overall progress is very important, because action plans often do not show the obvious hallmarks of progress that are apparent for activities such as designing, building a prototype, or conducting a test. In addition, action plans may not be as interesting to work on as these more "mainline" activities, and they do not contribute directly to shipping the product—but if they don't occur, they can definitely prevent shipping of the product.

KEY IDEA

Consequently, your action plans may fall to second priority easily—and in a heated environment, this means *no* priority. It is your job as project manager to ensure that you can measure progress on each plan and that you do this at least as often as you measure progress on anything else.

To quantify your progress, you will need to assess what has changed in the drivers and how these driver changes affect the risk's probabilities and total loss. This need not be a lengthy process, but it should be based on team consensus, not just an individual estimate by the project manager. Once you have these new values of probabilities and total loss for each managed risk, you are ready to chart your progress.

There are many ways of monitoring progress on your action plans. Your options depend on how you have chosen to prioritize your risks (see Chapter 6). If you are using a top 10 list, then you have reduced each risk to a single value, its expected loss. One way of portraying progress in reducing expected loss is shown in Figure 8-3. Notice that this chart conveys quickly to the team and management how well you are resolving each risk that is under management. For instance, progress on risk R5 was abrupt, when an action plan suddenly took effect, in contrast to risk R8, where progress was more progressive. Risk R3 actually reverted for a while.

When the expected loss reaches a threshold level, say four days on this chart, active management ends, and you can reassign the resources that have been devoted to managing this risk.

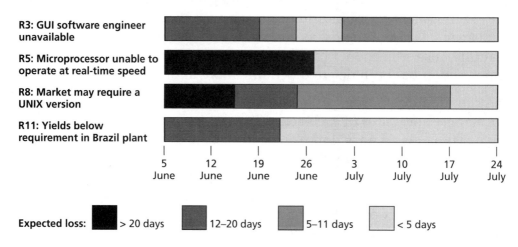

Figure 8-3. Tracking four of the risks on the top 10 list. The chart, shown at the end of the project (24 July), illustrates how the expected loss of each risk decreases over time. During the project, the chart would be blank to the right of the current date.

Alternatively, you may be using a risk map in place of or in conjunction with a top 10 list. In this case, you can plot progress in resolving the various risks directly on the risk map, as shown in Figure 8-4. If this map becomes cluttered with too many tracking lines, break the list of managed risks into groups using some convenient categories (such as sourcing, field trials, and production) and plot each category on its own map. Here again, the map provides a graphic display of how well you are progressing in managing your project's risks. Notice that this type of presentation also allows you to monitor risks that are not being actively managed now but might need action plans in the future if their underlying drivers or probabilities grow.

For either type of progress chart, you normally would review it at every team meeting and every project review. First, your team or the reviewers look at overall progress, using either the Figure 8-3 or Figure 8-4 chart. This may prompt questions about the progress of certain risks. Then you can go into the detailed activity of the risk resolution tasks using your more detailed risk task reports, as illustrated by Figure 8-2.

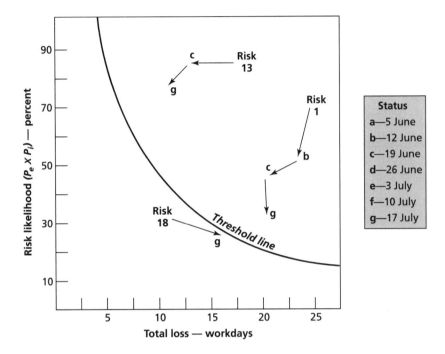

Figure 8-4. A risk map showing changes in both the total loss and the likelihood of three risks over a seven-week period. It also shows how close they are to changing states between "active" and "inactive." (Compare with Figure 3-3.)

Normally, you should monitor these action plans at the same interval as you monitor project financials, schedule, or open action items. Because your action plans are your safety net, monitoring them any less often than these other vital signs simply does not stand up to reason. In fact, your action plans are a predictive measure of other problems downstream. If your plans fall behind, risks will occur, and then you will have problems with the project financials or schedule. Thus, risk action plan status should be taken no less seriously than these other indicators of success.

KEY IDEA

TERMINATING ACTION PLANS FOR RISKS SUCCESSFULLY RESOLVED

Successful action plans require work and consume resources—risk management is not free! There is no point in continuing transference, avoidance, prevention, redundancy, or contingency plans beyond the point where they are needed. Consequently, your monitoring of plans should consider regularly which plans might be closed. If you are using a risk map, this will be obvious if you monitor progress on the map: watch for risks that fall below the threshold line. A top 10 list will not help, but a chart like Figure 8-3 will show you when to terminate your plan. Observe that, regardless of how many risks are actually on your top 10 list initially, at some point there will be fewer than 10 on the list as action plans terminate.

EXAMPLE

Your action plans will vary in termination details. Back in Chapter 3, we saw that a GUI software engineer might miss a software review due to field upgrades the engineer might have to perform at the time of the review. Perhaps your mitigation action was to arrange for someone else to make the field upgrades. Consequently, when the software review is over, make sure that you notify the person on call as a backup for the field upgrades. An example with more serious consequences would be a redundancy plan to design a part using a new computer-aided design (CAD) system in parallel with another team designing the same part with your existing CAD system. Because it is costly to staff redundant teams, you will want to watch this situation closely and reassign one team as soon as possible.

KEY IDEA

Even if a particular action plan has achieved its goal but does not seem to be much of a burden, there are other benefits from terminating it. Explicitly doing so reinforces that you are serious about identifying major risks and taking action against them. By letting old risks remain, you dilute the attention you can focus on the remaining crucial ones. For instance, if you show management a list of risks and they notice that most of the risks have already been resolved, they are likely to misjudge the status of your project. This may make it more difficult to get the management support needed for fighting the few remaining serious risks.

You handle the termination of contingency plans differently than prevention plans. If the prevention plan has completely eliminated the possibility of the risk, then the contingency plan can be closed as well. If the prevention plan has reduced but not entirely eliminated the risk, you will have to decide whether to continue the contingency plan. As described in Chapter 7, this decision usually depends on the residual expected loss. There are two exceptions, however. One is when you have a catastrophic loss possibility. In this case, you might decide to retain the contingency plan because of the risk's large total loss, even though its probability of occurrence is now quite small. The other exception is when the cost of maintaining the plan outweighs the benefit it can provide, as explained in Chapter 7. Consider, for example, automobile insurance. When your car gets old, you may choose to discontinue its collision insurance because its cost is high relative to your car's current value, which limits what the insurance company would pay you in event of damage. This is the cost–benefit exception. On the other hand, you would not discontinue the liability insurance on your old car, because this risk remains potentially catastrophic.

IDENTIFYING NEW RISKS

Potentially, completely new risks could appear at any time, or new clues could suggest risks that you had overlooked before. Part of ongoing monitoring is to look regularly and explicitly for new risks. This needn't be a time-consuming process, as it was initially. Probably the best approach is to go through a prompt list routinely at team meetings. You could ask:

- Do any of the events that have transpired on this project since our last meeting suggest a risk?
- Has anything changed in our marketplace or the regulatory environment that suggests a risk to our project?
- Is there anything in national or international news that suggests a new risk to our project?

In product development projects, changes in product requirements or specifications represent a common source of new risks, a phenomenon commonly known as scope creep. Such changes come about because the customer or user environment truly changes, because the team was not diligent enough initially in understanding customer requirements, or because a competitor's offering illuminates a missing feature in your product. Consequently, be particularly sensitive to changes in the marketplace, customers, or product usage when you conduct your ongoing risk identification. Also, remember when you analyze these scope-change risks that they often extend beyond the apparent change to disrupt completed parts of the project that you had until then considered to be low risk.

Depending on your organization and its needs, you can find effective ways of scanning your environment to discover new risks. Consider two techniques used by the Product Development Group at Battelle (Columbus, Ohio). This PDG develops products under contract for clients. For each development project, the PDG forms an advisory board whose members have specific experience that might apply to this project. For example, a project that includes complex manufacturing will include someone with such experience. These "outsiders" are not involved in the day-to-day details of the project and thus see project risks from a very different, broader viewpoint than does the project team. Due to the importance of the PDG's link with the client, they take this approach one step further. The advisory board includes an appointed chair who is responsible specifically for maintaining contact with the client's management and the client's project leadership. The chair is expected to have a sense of the state of mind of the client's management, based not only on talking with them but also on such things as watching financial and business news about the company. In addition to interacting with the client's management, the chair is also in touch with the client's project leadership, which provides a parallel communication path back to Battelle's development team. Many of PDG's clients have adopted the advisory board approach for their own internal projects.

If a new risk appears, you determine its impact and enter it on the tracking spreadsheet you started during the original risk identification step (see Chapter 4) so that you can monitor it. Next, assign a small group to analyze the risk to determine its risk event and impact drivers, probabilities of risk event and impact, and total loss. Depending on the resulting expected loss, this newly identified risk either moves on to receive action plans or is marked inactive because it does not now meet the criterion for active management.

As suggested, the steps for a new risk are simply a condensed version of those conducted initially and already described in Chapters 4 through 7. For instance, initially all project risks were analyzed in a rather large, formal workshop setting. For a new risk, you instead employ a small, cross-functional group that works informally. It is important to use a cross-functional group to overcome the biases and blind spots that an individual is likely to possess.

INITIATING NEW ACTION PLANS

New action plans arise from two sources: previously known risks whose importance has risen above the threshold for having action plans, and just-identified risks whose rated importance indicates that they require active management. The planning process is the same as before: assign a small group to develop action plans, fit the plans into your task structure, and obtain any additional resources you will need to execute them.

This completes our discussion of the process of monitoring project risks. Figure 8-5 illustrates how the various risk-monitoring activities fit together. Before each meeting or review, you normally complete the left box. These documents form the basis for the discussion in the second box. Then make sure to complete each of the three streams on the right.

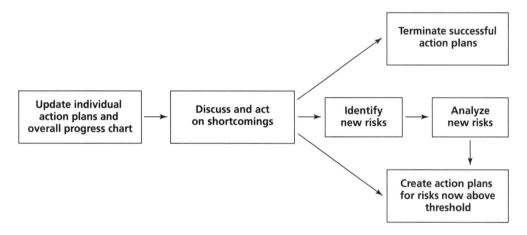

Figure 8-5. Components of risk monitoring, which are completed regularly at each team meeting and project review.

Communication

The cornerstone of any management system is effective communication; risk management is no exception. To review, the basic communication process comprises four critical components: sender, message, receiver, and feedback. In the realm of risk management, the project manager and the product development team must emphasize all of these components equally to ensure effective risk communications. This is particularly important in risk management because many executive managers have become accustomed to receiving only *reactive* data on risks that have already occurred, which usually means that people communicate only existing

KEY IDEA

crisis situations. However, if you pursue proactive risk management, you will find that your messages to executive managers will concentrate on the future and preparations for it. As you progress through the risk management process, you inform the team and your executive managers on the results of risk identification, analysis, prioritization and mapping, resolution planning, and monitoring. Except for some monitoring items, these steps involve risk messages *before* risk events occur.

As you have followed the risk management process throughout this book, we have continually emphasized effective communication with your team members to ensure that they understand the strategies followed and decisions made regarding risk management. This puts the team in a strong position to deliver messages, which may be transmitted in the form of risk management reports, metrics, or even the tracking spreadsheet you initiated in Chapter 4.

PRODUCT DEVELOPMENT TEAM COMMUNICATION

KEY IDEA

Team meetings should always set risk management as a top focus, because risk items are often the cause of the schedule and cost problems that normally become the top focus. We recommend that the project manager use meeting minutes, the risk tracking spreadsheet, and the risk map as tools to help communicate the risk message to the product development team. During team meetings, the project manager should ensure that the following are reviewed:

- progress on action plans for the prioritized risk list (top 10 list),
- changes to the probability estimates,
- any necessary changes to risk action plans,
- any upcoming triggers for prevention and contingency plans,
- any resolved risks closing,
- risks that are below the threshold line on the risk map, determining if the data has changed enough to place them on the prioritized risk list, and
- new risks that may be arising, especially if a risk event has occurred (it may become a driver for another risk event).

Besides these regular team meetings, you will be communicating daily with individuals on specific risks.

Risk Management Metrics

Metrics have become a popular management topic over the past several years. Handled well, they have great power to improve your business performance over time. Managed poorly, they can cause harm by encouraging counterproductive behavior and creating distrust and cynicism within your teams.

Companies that get the greatest value from metrics are open about collecting them, sharing the results, discussing their implications, and taking action on the findings. Hewlett-Packard is one example of such a company (see Grady in "Supplementary Reading"). To make this point more clearly, we show you what not to do. The first "not" is to collect the numbers and not share them with employees. Employees will gradually wonder why they are spending their time reporting their numbers. Worse, they may become concerned that their numbers will be used against them. In this information vacuum, employees may even collect their own metrics to manage their careers.

CAUTION

The second "not" is not to discuss results broadly throughout the organization. Metrics are seldom pure measures, and various people will have various views on what they mean, yielding a richer interpretation. In addition, when it comes time to improve business practices or processes based on your metrics, previous discussions will have paved the way for change.

This leads to the last "not," not taking action. This is where employees can become cynical. If the numbers consistently show that certain changes should be made, but management stalls on making those changes, the organization would have been better off not collecting metrics in the first place.

Our conclusion: although metrics can be a wonderful tool for improving performance, work out your metrics philosophy beforehand to ensure a positive result. In addition, remember that when you share and discuss metrics, behavior is likely to adapt to the metric. By just communicating metrics results broadly, people will start thinking of ways to improve the numbers without even having an official improvement initiative. The negative side of this phenomenon is that people can "game" the metrics to improve what the numbers say about them, without actually improving your business objective. Again, think carefully about the goals and ramifications of your metrics program before you implement it.

Also, assure that your metrics are reasonably balanced. For instance, if you collect and advertise *only* metrics that emphasize how many risks you precluded, people might start believing that risk is *always* bad and respond by becoming risk averse and overly conservative with their risk management. You can balance this tendency by also advertising what it is costing (in time, money, or another objective) to preclude risks or by showing which risks became opportunities.

Metrics is an important subject that goes beyond the scope of this book. A full metrics program can consume great amounts of resources, and some companies devote a great deal of attention to metrics. This is an area where you have to decide how far to go and which metrics pay off *for you*. There is no standard prescription. Consequently, we provide here several guidelines and an example of a rather thorough application of metrics to project risk management.

KEY IDEA

We prefer to break metrics into two categories, each having different objectives and techniques. *Strategic metrics* provide you with long-term trends aggregated over many projects to overcome the inevitable project-to-project variation. They answer the question, "Is our organization improving since we started measuring our risk management performance?" In contrast, *tactical metrics* apply on a project-by-project basis. They answer the question, "Is our team managing risk well on this project?" Strategic metrics, to be useful, must remain stable enough to detect trends. Tactical metrics, conversely, should be adapted to the needs of the project at hand. Except for a few measures that may feed into strategic metrics at the end of the project, they will be useful only during the project, perhaps only during a small portion of it.

STRATEGIC METRICS

KEY IDEA

Strategic metrics detect long-term changes. This is especially important for project risk management, because improvements are likely to be forgotten. Unless you track the numbers, an average project schedule slip of two weeks may seem ordinary today, but your metrics could tell you that it was eight weeks five years ago, when you started your project risk management program. Two weeks is not natural; eight weeks is what it would naturally be. If management decides to eliminate project risk management, allows it to wane, or reverts to firefighting, you can expect that your average schedule slip will return to eight weeks. An appropriate set of long-term metrics is the best survival insurance available for your risk management program.

The objective of a project risk management program is usually to eliminate project schedule and budget overruns, because other difficulties, such as product quality, performance, or cost problems ultimately result in schedule or budget problems. Consequently, the most obvious strategic metrics are measures of schedule and budget performance relative to plan. If you change your plan during the course of the project, you will have to decide whether to base your metrics on the original plan or the modified one. This decision should stem clearly from your business objectives—in other words, what really matters to the business. If other parameters such as product quality, product cost, or product performance are more fundamental to your business objectives, track them instead.

The problem with such top-level metrics is that, although they measure exactly what you are trying to improve, many factors besides project risk management (such as skills, strategy, and market volatility) can influence schedule and budget performance. Consequently, track these metrics, but also track more specific ones tying directly to project risk management.

CAUTION

Two strategic metrics measure the effectiveness of your project risk management program. The first is risks identified and averted due to your risk management. This number should be readily available by examining your risk management list at the end of each project. Based on the nature of your projects, you will have to decide whether to use the absolute values (risks averted over all projects for the organization) or some kind of relative measure (risks averted per project, or percent of risks identified that were averted).

The other strategic project risk metric—probably the more valuable one—is risks that went unidentified but later occurred. This takes more effort to measure. At the end of each project, conduct a post-project review (see Chapter 11 for details) and specifically identify the unanticipated negative events that happened during the project. Then ask whether each of these risk events was identifiable before it occurred, either at the beginning of the project or during your regular risk management monitoring. Besides just the number of such unidentified risks, note some details of the risk events so that you can put them in categories and start seeking patterns of such risks. Once you see the pattern, you can probably discover a way to detect such risks proactively in the future. In this way, you not only collect the metric, but also discover the means for overcoming the largest contributors to it.

TACTICAL METRICS

KEY IDEA

Executives, project managers, and product development teams use tactical metrics as a means for determining the risk management status of the project. We consider these metrics to be "in process" since they are designed to be used throughout the project as you move forward.

EXAMPLE Figure 8-6 is an example of how you can use tactical metrics to determine if your risk management activities are effective. This "dashboard" helps the product development team monitor the current risk situation and the progress they have made. We are highlighting these risk metrics as examples that could be used, but we encourage you and your teams to adjust these metrics as you grow and evolve your own risk management metrics system. Meyer (see article in "Supplementary Reading") makes the point that such dashboards should be simple and quick to interpret, with only a few key "instruments," just like dashboards in a car. For instance, Meyer drives racecars, and he observes that in a street car, the speedometer is the largest and most important instrument, for good reason. But racecars do not even have speedometers, because speed limits make no sense in a race.

As you consider tools such as dashboards, think about how you can automate data collection and the presentation. These tools can require considerable effort to keep up to date, but modern networking and data-processing methods can help greatly if applied appropriately.

In the following sections, we describe each metric in Figure 8-6, showing you how to interpret the information being conveyed. Overall, notice that this dashboard is arranged with numbers of risks at the top and losses at the bottom, trends on the left and current values on the right. Along with the dashboard, the tracking spreadsheet used throughout the risk manage-

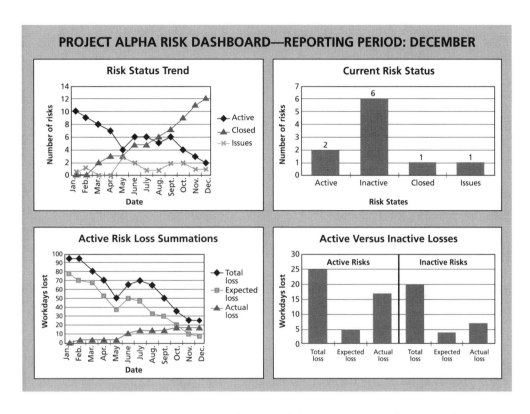

Figure 8-6. A risk management dashboard shows the status of project risks.

ment process and the risk map described in Chapter 6 can all be integral to the project manager's risk management toolkit.

RISK STATUS TREND

The upper left quadrant of Figure 8-6 shows a trend chart monitoring the active, issue, and closed risk status states. These metrics provide insight on how well you are preventing risks from becoming issues and how effective you are at closing risks. This chart is only monitoring risks the team members placed on the top 10 list. (In the following paragraphs, we cover how to monitor the risks that are not on this list.)

This chart monitors three pieces of data:

* number of active risks being managed for each reporting period,

- number of issues (resulting from active risks) for each reporting period, and
- cumulative count of closed risks.

To determine if risks are being prevented, review the number of issues being managed for your reporting period. The preferred trend is to reduce the number of issues being managed. If the number is too high in relation to the number of active risks, then you have not been preventing risks from occurring adequately. Another objective is steady growth in the number of closed risks. The number of active risks should remain steady (assuming that you are adding risks to your prioritized list as you close others) or preferably, decline over each reporting period. If your active list grows, your initial risk identification workshops might have been inadequate.

CURRENT RISK STATUS

The upper right quadrant of Figure 8-6 provides a synopsis of current risk management status. The active and issue bars come from the current values of the trend chart. The closed bar shows the risks closed during the last period, rather than the cumulative closures. And the inactive bar is data new to the figure. This bar chart allows you to make some additional observations. For instance, generally you should have fewer issues being managed than risks. If there are more issues than risks, you should be concerned about the quality of your prevention plans. (Remember that this counts only the issues that result from risks that were formerly active. You are likely to have many other open issues in your project not connected with these risks.)

ACTIVE RISK LOSS SUMMATIONS

The lower left quadrant of Figure 8-6 shows a trend chart for loss values. In addition to the sum of total losses and expected losses for all risks on your top 10 list, the chart shows the cumulative actual losses experienced when both risk events and their impacts occur. This metric indicates how effective your action plans are in managing total, expected, and actual losses on the top 10 list. The team could duplicate this metric for the inactive risks too, but we prefer to use the comparison bar chart covered in the next section.

This results-oriented metric provides the final judgment on whether or not risk management is effective. Total loss should either stay steady (assuming you continually add risks to your top 10 list as you close others) or gradually decline as you close risks. The expected loss should continually trend downward as the effects of prevention and contingency reduce the probabilities of the risk event and impact, respectively. The true test will be the cumulative actual loss experienced by the team. This value will trend upward as the project progresses because, even with your best efforts, some risks will still occur. Some risks could be unknown to the team, and by the time they surface it may be too late to take effective action.

KEY IDEA

ACTIVE VERSUS INACTIVE LOSSES

The lower right quadrant of Figure 8-6 contrasts loss values for both active and inactive risks. This chart is a "snapshot" of losses for the current reporting period. You can see that the active risk losses appearing on the left half are simply the most recent values from the trend lines in the lower left quadrant of the dashboard. The right half of this snapshot illustrates corresponding losses for the inactive risks.

This chart allows you to ascertain whether the risks on the prioritized list are the most significant ones. Compare the active and inactive risks. The total loss bars are not too significant, but if you have selected the "right" risks to manage actively, your active expected loss should be greater than your inactive expected loss. If not, then you should reassess how you prioritized your risks. Similarly, if the actual loss for the inactive list exceeds that for the active list, you have probably chosen the wrong risks to manage. Unfortunately, because these risks have already happened, this insight is of little value for the current project; however, it is invaluable as a learning opportunity for future projects and for improving your risk identification workshops.

CAUTION

Adapt this dashboard example to your business and projects, being mindful of what will help you the most, fit your corporate culture, and be relatively easy to keep up to date with the data-processing tools available to you. If you do use a dashboard as comprehensive as this one, the need to train your team and your management in reading it should be apparent by now.

Running Example—Conclusion

We now reach the conclusion of our running example, in which Bernardo is worried about having a heart attack. This hypothetical example is meant only to illustrate the risk management techniques described in this book. We do not intend that anyone use this example as a medical reference or modify any personal behavior based on this data.

Up to this point, Bernardo has identified the risk he is worried about, analyzed the risk, and prioritized and developed risk action plans to mitigate his likelihood of having a heart attack. With his action plans defined, he now needs to determine how to monitor the risks and the surrounding data.

Recall his prevention plans. His first actions to stave off a heart attack were to enroll in a stress management course and request a less stressful job function. The question arises, how does he monitor the effectiveness of these plans? Since Bernardo is trying to reduce stress, one way to monitor would be to take periodic blood pressure measurements. As stress diminishes, he should see a reduction in his blood pressure levels.

His next prevention plan was designed to change the fact that Bernardo does not get exercise and is overweight. He started with a visit to his physician to evaluate his health. This can be used to set a baseline for his blood pressure and weight metrics. He also met with the physician to set up an exercise and diet program. So how does he monitor effectiveness? He can monitor his resting heart rate, which should diminish as he progresses with his exercise program. To monitor his diet, he simply can monitor his weight. If the exercise program and diet are being effective, his weight should decrease. As Bernardo got into his program, he found that maintaining his diet was particularly difficult. So, in addition to his monthly weight and blood pressure readings (strategic metrics to track trends), he weighed himself daily for a while and posted the results on his refrigerator door—an excellent tactical metric to change his eating behavior.

Bernardo understands the nature of risk management. He recognizes that even with the best of prevention plans, he still may have a heart attack. Thus, he has developed contingency plans to mitigate the consequences. His first strategy was to work with the village trustees to acquire better medical services for the local community. However, because the government entity might not take action in an expeditious fashion, this contingency plan might have minimal affect on the likelihood of dying from a heart attack in the short term, even though Bernardo was still pursuing it.

Another contingency plan related to the fact that his spouse did not drive. His plan was to teach his spouse to drive in case he had to be driven to medical facilities. When his spouse received her license, it had a positive effect by reducing the probability of impact.

The final contingency plan addressed the loss of income his spouse would experience in the event of his death. Note that this contingency plan does nothing to mitigate the likelihood of death—his stated impact—but serves only to minimize the financial effect on his spouse. We use similar contingencies in projects in terms of schedule buffers and monetary reserves. The buffers and reserves do nothing to mitigate the impacts of risks, but they do protect our final delivery dates or budgets.

Figure 8-7 is an updated version of the standard risk model five years later, with the new risk drivers and reduced probabilities for the risk event and impact. As you can see, Bernardo has been successful in reducing the overall risk of the heart attack. As it turns out, he has reduced his expected loss

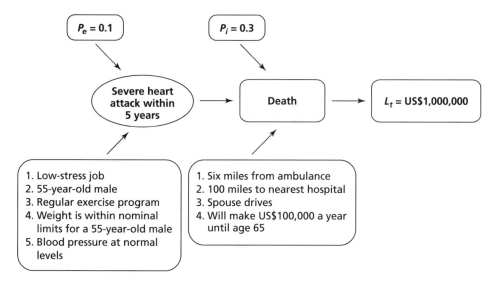

Figure 8-7. Heart attack example with updated drivers that changed as a result of action plans. This is the state of the risk five years after the risk was first identified. Compare with Figure 5-7.

Table 8-1. Final outcomes of Bernardo's action plans at the end of five years.

Prevention Plans	Outcomes
Take stress management courses starting on June 13.	Successfully completed stress management course. Blood pressure readings have decreased.
Request to be re-assigned to a different job function.	Re-assigned to a different department, which has lower stress levels. Blood pressure readings have decreased.
Schedule appointment for June 3 with doctor for health evaluation and to develop a safe exercise program.	Completed exam with the doctor who cleared Bernardo for an exercise program.
Starting on June 10 an exercise program will be initiated.	Exercise program has been successful in reducing the resting heart rate and significantly reducing his weight.
Schedule appointment for June 3 with doctor for health evaluation and to develop a safe diet program.	Completed exam with the doctor who developed a safe diet for Bernardo.
Starting on June 10 a doctor-supervised diet will be started.	The diet has been successful in helping to reducing weight to acceptable levels for a 55-year-old male.
Contingency Plans	**Outcomes**
Work with village trustees to acquire an ambulance service.	One year after the initiating this contingency plan, the village trustees were successful in acquiring ambulance service to support the community.
Place house for sale on June 3 and move closer to a larger city.	Plan not implemented since Bernardo's family is located near his current home.
Work with village trustees to acquire an immediate care facility.	Five years after initiating this contingency plan, the village trustees were not successful in acquiring an immediate care facility to support the community due to lack of village funds.
Schedule driving lessons for spouse. Current cost estimates are US$25 an hour, but the closest place to give driving lessons is 50 miles from the village.	Due to the distance and cost of getting these driving lessons, the subject opted not to pursue this plan.
Starting on June 4, I will provide driving lessons for my spouse. We are targeting to complete the lessons by July 9. We have an appointment scheduled for July 16 for the driving exam.	Bernardo taught his spouse to drive over a course of six weeks. At the conclusion of the training, the spouse successfully passed the state exam for driving.
Take out life insurance policy equal to the value of the expected loss.	A 15-year-term life insurance policy was taken out by Bernardo to cover lost salary in the event of his death.

from US$525,000 to US$30,000. Some of this improvement is simply due to the fact that he is five years closer to retirement now, but even if this did not change, his expected loss would have decreased from US$525,000 to US$45,000. To close on this example, we have included Table 8-1 as the final outcome of each of his action plans.

Summary

Risk monitoring is the oversight that the project manager and team place on the risk management process. Monitoring is a crucial component of the process because it allows you to ascertain that the whole program is working. Specifically, a risk metrics dashboard shows you whether your action plans are truly controlling the effects of uncertainty on your project. Effective monitoring will show whether the probabilities are dropping, and if they are not dropping, the same monitoring scheme should indicate how to make corrections. When you have identified a resolution plan that is not working, you should take corrective action and develop another strategy.

Supplementary Reading

Brown, Mark Graham. *Keeping Score.* Portland, Oregon: Productivity, Inc, 1996. A practical handbook on performance metrics. Although he is oriented toward broad-scale corporate metrics programs, Brown offers valuable advice on constructing and using many types of metrics.

Grady, Robert B. *Practical Software Metrics for Project Management and Process Improvement.* Englewood Cliffs, New Jersey: Prentice-Hall, 1992. This is the first author we know of to divide metrics into strategic and tactical categories. Although oriented toward software projects, by drawing on his experience working at Hewlett-Packard, Grady provides valuable insights on strategic metrics.

Meyer, Christopher. How the right measures help teams excel. *Harvard Business Review* 72(3): 95–103 (1994). Excellent source on tactical metrics—emphasizing dashboards—that a product development team can use to improve its own performance.

9
RISK MANAGEMENT TOOLKIT

Chapters 4 through 8 describe a complete risk management process, and Chapter 3 provides an overview of this process. As you work through the various phases of the process, however, you may find the tools in this chapter to be helpful. These tools only *support* your risk management process (often only in special cases); they are not a substitute for it.

We start with two tools that you can apply generally to the risk management process, and then describe three special-purpose tools useful for understanding specific risks that are unusually complex or significant:

- sticky density, which is useful for pinpointing risky areas in a process, project, or organization;
- spreadsheets, which you can use in countless ways to organize, analyze, sort, or present your project risk data;
- decision analysis, a tool helpful in understanding situations involving uncertainty;
- risk simulation, which allows you to see the overall effects of multiple risks; and
- design structure matrix, useful for unraveling the type of iterative processes that occur in product development, in which risks arise from not having certain information until after you need it.

Sticky Density

We used the sticky density technique in Chapter 4 to assist in the risk identification workshop. The objective in that workshop was for the product development team to develop a visual aid to focus on the "risky" areas of their schedule. More generally, the value of this tool is to highlight potential problem areas associated with interdependencies between functional areas or different parts of a process. The goal of the tool is to help the team discover problem areas where risk seems to be concentrated.

STICKY DENSITY FOR RISK IDENTIFICATION

Before starting to identify risks using sticky density, prepare adequately. You will need to develop a network diagram of the schedule or process that you would like to analyze. Next, you will need several pads of stickies, one for each team member invited to the workshop. You might be able to use different colored stickies to signify something about the problem being analyzed, such as internal versus contractor or supplier risk. However, we recommend against giving each member a different color, because once the stickies are placed they should belong to the team, not individuals.

Select participants who have contributed directly to the development of the network diagram. Distribute to them a copy of the network diagram, along with instructions to review the material and come to the workshop prepared to identify potential problem areas. Prior to the workshop, post the network diagram on the wall (alternatively, you can simply use a whiteboard with the diagram hand drawn). The important point is to make the picture big enough for all to see and for patches of stickies to be localized on the diagram.

Once the session has started, the facilitator walks through every element comprising the network diagram and requests that the team, "List any unique interactions that may disrupt this particular partition/element." Instruct participants to write down any risks they identify on their stickies and post them on the network diagram (if you are conducting a risk identification workshop, you will need to capture both the risk event and its impact).

RETROSPECTIVE APPLICATION TO ROOT CAUSES

We have also found this technique useful when performing root-cause analysis to determine why a particular risk event occurred, or worse, why the total loss occurred despite contingency plans being in place. As you may recall from Chapter 2, we mentioned that the Ishikawa Risk Model is helpful for performing retrospectives. The sticky density technique can be used in conjunction with this model to assist in developing a root cause. To use this technique, you gather all the relevant data for the particular risk event that occurred and then convert the data to the form of the Ishikawa Risk Model. Participants individually list on their stickies why they believe the risk event and impact occurred. You can jump-start the analysis effort by using the 4 Ps: people, process, product, and performance. The 4 Ps represent potential risk events that contribute to the cause of the risk. As individuals complete their stickies, they post them on the Ishikawa model.

GENERAL GUIDANCE ON THE STICKY DENSITY TECHNIQUE

This type of workshop requires some facilitation skill. The facilitator should check the statement on each sticky to ensure that it is clear and responds to the question asked. When analyzing for risks in schedules, we have found it helpful to proceed by time interval, such as weekly or monthly. If you are analyzing a process, it is best to review that process one box at a time. Note that a sticky is not required for every conceivable risk, but you do want to discover those risks that have the greatest potential to disrupt your project's goals.

After the facilitator completes the walk-through of the entire diagram, step back and observe the network diagram for any "sticky densities." If you see a cluster (or clusters) around a particular time interval, interaction, or process step, the team can focus on this area to be corrected or resolved. Figure 9-1 provides an example of a finished sticky diagram. In addition, if you find an isolated sticky, you should query the individual who wrote it: he or she may know something the rest of the team does not.

At the conclusion of the workshop, consolidate your stickies, particularly those that were in a high "sticky density" area. If this is a risk identification workshop, the stickies will become your risk events and impacts, and you can then move on to the next part of the risk management process. If you are analyzing a risk that occurred previously, or a process, assign owners or a team to correct the situation and bring a solution back for the others to review and approve.

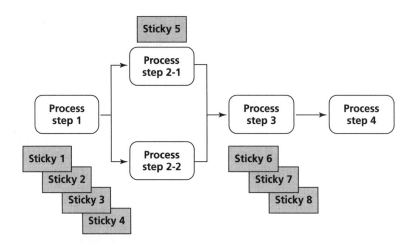

Figure 9-1. This simplified example shows how the stickies have been overlayed onto a process, drawing attention to areas of concern.

This technique's primary benefits are that it requires no special equipment, it is inexpensive, and most importantly, it is a team-based activity that allows each participant to contribute to the process. As such, it is excellent for building team consensus on areas of focus for further analysis, especially when several risks interact in a small area. As with any technique, you should exercise some caution, however, because a solo risk that fails to draw attention can in fact be the most serious one.

Spreadsheets

Spreadsheets are the mainstay of any project manager's toolkit. A spreadsheet can be an effective means to document and monitor the status of project risks that your team may be facing, or be used as a database to monitor resource allocation on projects.

For example, Figure 8-2 is a tracking form for a particular risk. It captures relevant information from the risk management process that can be used to communicate the status of a risk to the project team. (Throughout Chapters 4 through 8, we advised you to record your data at the end of each step.) Figure 8-1 shows how this form can be combined with other worksheets to track all risks for a project. The project team is responsible for keeping the spreadsheet up to date; however, we usually recommend that the project manager (or his or her equivalent) retain ownership of the spreadsheet. A primary focus for project team meetings should be reviewing the spreadsheet that tracks your managed risks.

Figures 8-1 and 8-2 are relatively formal spreadsheets. Spreadsheets are also invaluable for quick analyses, organizing personal action items, tracking test results, and similar tasks.

The benefit of using a spreadsheet multiplies when you must develop charts and graphs to present your risk management results to others (Figure 8-6 provides a sample of charts made from spreadsheets). With all levels of industry having ready access to spreadsheets, there is no excuse for not presenting data in a form easy for all to comprehend. Chapter 8 provides detailed information on metrics, along with spreadsheet charts to present them.

Some software packages are coming into use for project risk management and the product development process. These have their place, but they will not replace the spreadsheet, the extreme flexibility of which will always be useful for quick analyses and special situations.

Decision Analysis

Decision analysis is your "Swiss Army knife" of risk management. Schuyler (see "Supplementary Reading" at the end of this chapter) calls it a "discipline for helping decision makers choose wisely under conditions of uncertainty." We think of it as more of a graphical technique to help you organize your thoughts and reach agreement on a relatively complex situation involving uncertainty.

In this section, we lead off with a broad explanation of the decision analysis methodology and various ways in which you can apply it. Refer to Figure 9-2, which portrays the analysis of a particular risk. Once you understand how decision analysis works, we provide a risk management example. You may wish to start with the example. Then please return here, because the value of decision analysis for project risk management resides more in a general appreciation of its versatility and power than in a complete understanding of this example.

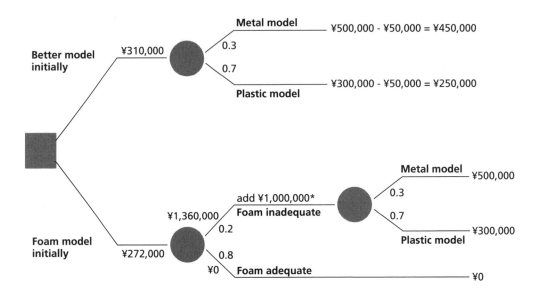

Figure 9-2. Decision analysis tree for analyzing and planning a risk of not providing a good enough model of the product at a review.

DECISION ANALYSIS METHODOLOGY

As the figure demonstrates, decision analysis is portrayed as a decision tree and is usually laid out chronologically from left to right, like a project management network (PERT/CPM) diagram. By convention, circles represent splits out of your control and squares indicate decisions that you can make. To the right of each circle, the tree shows the probability associated with that branch, and it lists outcomes quantitatively at the far right end of the branch.

Although you read the tree from left to right chronologically, you perform the calculations from right to left. For example, the ¥310,000 (Japanese yen) at the top of the tree is the value at this point. It is the result of 0.3 × ¥450,000 + 0.7 × ¥250,000, working from the right. Similarly, the middle branch computes to ¥360,000, plus the ¥1,000,000, yields the ¥1,360,000.

The basis of Figure 9-2 is monetary, but you can use any other quantity consistently as a basis. For analyzing project risks, the basic unit will most likely be days or weeks of project delay. If you do use a monetary basis and have an unusually long project, you can use net present values (NPV)—usually relative to the left end of the tree—to account for the time value of money. In addition, for a long project, incorporate incremental funding, which is usually more realistic and fits well with the decision analysis methodology.

You can even draw the tree without a basis quantity. Then, all quantities on the tree are probabilities, and the calculation rules at the nodes will differ depending on how the probabilities combine. This can be useful for determining your probabilities of risk event or impact. Although you will normally just estimate such probabilities using the group consensus of your team, in more complex cases you may find that you can do better by using a tree structure to break the probability down into its components, estimating the components, and then computing the final probability.

KEY IDEA

Observe that the value of decision analysis resides in its ability to really "think through" a situation, as an individual or as a group, to see how the components fit together. Often, you can break the situation down into elements that are easier to estimate, or you discover alternatives or logical flaws that were not apparent until you laid out the structure. Consequently, use this tool to structure your thoughts quickly by sketching the situation on a pad, white board, or flip chart—or their electronic equivalents for "virtual" meetings. This can be useful when:

- it is easier to estimate the components than the composite;
- there is uncertainty, confusion, or disagreement regarding the underlying structure, components, or options;
- the consequences of an error in assessment could be catastrophic;
- you need another way to approach a situation when you have reached an impasse; and/or
- you suspect that you are not considering everything or that you have some bias.

Finally, notice that the results computed toward the left side of the tree are weighted averages (or speaking more technically, expected values). This is usually appropriate because it tells you what will happen—on average.

However, if you seek a worst-case outcome, you can draw a similar tree but aggregate it differently by choosing the worst case at each split.

DECISION ANALYSIS EXAMPLE

EXAMPLE Figure 9-2 portrays this identified risk: when the team gets to a certain review, the marketing group will decide that the team's physical model is inadequate for making a decision regarding acceptability of the product attributes of shape, feel, looks, or ergonomics—thus delaying the project while a better model is built. When they planned the project, the team assumed a basic (foam) model, which is adequate normally. But now, due to the complexity of this product, they see the foam model as a risk. Consequently, they are considering avoiding this risk by reversing the earlier decision on the foam model and building a better model instead. Because they are starting with the foam model, they calculate costs relative to its cost.

The tree has two major branches for planning the resolution of this risk: the lower one, to build an inexpensive foam model initially and hope that it will be adequate; and the upper one, to build a better model initially to avoid the risk. The team judges that there is an 80 percent probability (0.8 on the tree) that the foam model will be adequate. But if it fails to be adequate, they will have to make either a solid plastic model or a metal one to satisfy marketing, as well as suffer a one-week (¥1,000,000) project delay while the better model is built and evaluated. Observe that the ¥272,000 is the expected loss for this risk.

Alternatively, the team could invest initially in a better model. Although either type of better model would be more expensive (either ¥500,000 or ¥300,000), they could save the ¥50,000 expense of the foam model. The decision analysis, at this state of refinement, suggests that they should accept the risk that the foam model would be inadequate and proceed with building it, because the cost of avoiding it outweighs the expected loss of the risk. This illustrates that avoiding a known risk is not always the wisest strategy.

Notice that the team could refine this model further by recognizing that, if they went with the better model initially, they could *choose* either the metal or the plastic one. Then the upper circle would become a square. For the plastic-model branch from this square, there would now be a chance that even a plastic model would not satisfy marketing, so they could add a circle to the plastic-model branch to model this uncertainty. They could also include a cost of delay if marketing would not accept a plastic model, as was done on the *Foam inadequate* branch of the figure.

Risk Simulation

Risk simulation is considered a mature and effective method to analyze project risks. Done correctly, risk simulation can put the Standard Risk Model into "motion." That is, you can incorporate the risk data into a comprehensive schedule of the project to develop an accurate forecast of the project completion date. If you are quantifying your losses in terms other than time, such as budget, product cost, or product performance, you can also apply risk simulation to them.

Risk simulation tools can increase your confidence level regarding your project completion date. Given the uncertainty of innovation, your ability to predict the exact date of completion is nearly impossible. Risk simulation tools fill in the completion picture by providing detailed information on how likely the project is to be completed by various dates. During risk analysis you only developed a total loss value with a single probability; however, simulation allows you to use probability distribution curves for individual tasks. For example, you may estimate that you have a 25 percent chance of completing a task in 120 days, a 50 percent chance of making it in 144 days, and a 90 percent chance of finishing in 187 days. Once you have developed such probability distribution estimates, you insert them into your risk simulation tool.

A simple example of risk simulation will show how it works. Figure 9-3 is EXAMPLE a Gantt chart depicting five tasks from a project. We have exact task duration estimates for two of the five tasks, Task IDs 2 and 4. The remaining three tasks have typically varied in duration on past projects, but we have a good idea of the range. For example, Task ID 3 has historically required at least 3 days, most often lasted 5 days, and at worst has taken 10 days. Risk simulation idealizes the probability surrounding these three dates by using what is known as a triangular probability distribution (see Grey's book in "Supplementary Reading" for details), and it does the same for the

ID	Task name	Start	Finish	Duration	Probability distribution		8/4	8/11	8/18	8/25	9/1	9/8
1	Test software project	Aug. 1	Sept. 3	24d								
2	Identify defects to correct	Aug. 1	Aug. 5	3d								
3	Correct sofware defects	Aug. 6	Aug. 12	5d	Triangle (3d, 5d, 10d)							
4	Build software load	Aug. 13	Aug. 13	1d								
5	Perform integration tests	Aug. 14	Aug. 20	5d	Triangle (3d, 5d, 7d)							
6	Perform validation tests	Aug. 21	Sept. 3	10d	Triangle (5d, 10d, 15d)							

Figure 9-3. Simple example to illustrate how probability functions can be integrated into a project management tool to allow risk simulation.

other two tasks subject to variation, one using a triangle of 3 days, 5 days, and 7 days, and the other using a triangle of 5 days, 10 days, and 15 days.

Risk simulation typically uses a process known as Monte Carlo analysis. It picks a number at random, falling within the probability distributions you have chosen, for each of the variable tasks. Then it runs through the schedule using these numbers to calculate the completion date. Next, it picks another set of random numbers for the variable tasks and recalculates the schedule. The simulation may repeat this process a thousand times to arrive at a representative picture of the completion date. It is called Monte Carlo because of the repeated random samplings, reminiscent of gambling.

Figure 9-4 shows corresponding results from a risk simulation tool (a commercially available computer package). This is a cumulative probability distribution curve. The chart shows how uncertainty in three of the task duration estimates affects the project finish dates. For instance, you have a 50-50 chance of finishing by September 4 and a 100 percent chance by September 18 (reading from the "triangular" curve; we explain the other curve shortly). You can readily see the value of this type of chart, particularly when you need to brief executives at a program review. However, it is up to the product development team to effectively manage the risks that lead to uncertainty in task duration. Normally, we recommend that you develop action plans to reduce the *probability* of a particular event, but when you are using risk simulation with a triangular distribution, you should reduce uncertainty in the *duration*. Otherwise, your next simulation will not improve the uncertainty in the project end date.

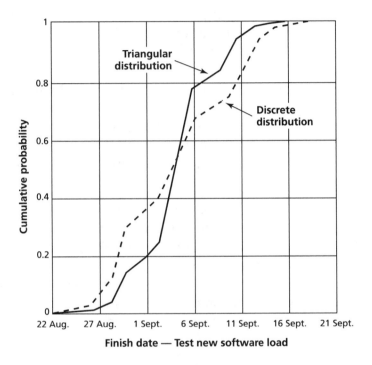

Finish date — Test new software load

Figure 9-4. Probability of finishing by a certain date. Two curves reflect two different assumptions for modeling the "correct defects" task duration.

As just suggested, there can be conceptual differences between our normal mode of analyzing risks by using their drivers and analyzing them using risk simulation. For instance, risk simulation allows you to use a triangular probability distribution—as discussed above—to portray your historical experience in completing a certain type of task, which models a minimum, a most likely, and a maximum task duration. If you look at the same task based only on the drivers for the current project, you might instead view it as a task that will take 3 days if there are no difficulties, but 10 days if the person assigned to it is committed to another project when he or she is needed (nothing in between, either 3 days or 10 days). You can

CAUTION

simulate such situations by using a discrete probability distribution instead of a triangular one. Figure 9-4 indicates the difference in results for the "correct defects" task. The conclusion is that you cannot apply these powerful tools blindly. You must appreciate what they are doing so that you can model what you believe is happening.

CAUTION

We have worked with several groups that decided they wanted to jump straight into risk simulation without understanding the risk management process. Without understanding the basics, these untrained people will encounter many problems when they attempt to use these tools. Risk simulation provides very detailed information about project risks, but remember the adage "garbage in, garbage out." We cannot emphasize enough that people must understand the entire risk management process before attempting to use risk simulation. Otherwise, you do a disservice to yourself and your company by providing a false sense of security from the results these tools suggest.

KEY IDEA

If you decide to use these tools, remember that they will take the subjective estimation data you provide and convert it to information. You must provide the intelligence to interpret what the information is telling you. In other words, the tool will not make decisions for you. We have seen too many examples of organizations believing tools will be the panacea to solve their problems. A risk simulation tool will not make decisions on how to manage risks, or even which project risks to manage.

Design Structure Matrix

Some risks do not have to be risks. Often, in creating a design process, developers unknowingly inject risks stemming from information unavailability. Each design task requires information from other tasks in order to be completed. When this information is available from an earlier task, the process works as planned, but when the information will come from a task that has yet to be completed, you have a problem.

EXAMPLE For example, if you were to design a potato peeler, its blade geometry would depend on what kind of potatoes you planned to peel (some varieties of potatoes are smoother and firmer than are others). But the range of potato types addressed will depend on how well the peeler works on various varieties, which, in turn, depends on blade geometry. To resolve this Catch-22, you must break the loop of dependency somewhere. For instance, you can simply assume some blade geometry values, make a peeler using them, peel a range of potatoes with it, and proceed from there repeatedly.

The objective of the design structure matrix (DSM) is to analyze the sequence of project activities in order to manage the not-yet-available information. When such information is needed, you can proceed only by making an assumption regarding it. Using the assumption, you can proceed to the following steps, but then you must return to verify whether the assumption you made still holds. If not, you revise the assumption and proceed until the assumption holds acceptably well. This process is called iteration. It introduces schedule and budget risks, because you have no idea in advance how many times you may have to iterate until you obtain an adequate result. Unfortunately, iteration is a hallmark of innovation, so you can expect to encounter it when you develop new products.

The DSM will help you to reduce iteration to its minimum and then to understand where any residual iteration will occur so that you can antici-pate it, thus reducing schedule risk. To some people, DSM refers to the same tool but means dependency structure matrix instead. In either case, it can be used to analyze any process, not just design processes. That is, "design" refers to designing a process, not to the design process.

KEY IDEA

You can use a DSM to analyze a process at three levels. First is the task level, as suggested in the previous few paragraphs: which task(s) must be a predecessor(s) of the current task? An alternative is the information level: which design parameter(s) do you need in order to calculate the present parameter? Operating at the information level has the advantage that information is more fundamental than tasks, so working at the information level tends to stabilize the problem definition. However, the weakness of working at the information level is that the results then have to be transformed to tasks in order to be useful for project plan-ning. The third level is the organization structure level, which we do not cover here.

EXAMPLE To show you how the DSM works, we provide an example, which is a simplification of the type of coffee maker commonly found in residences or hotel rooms. Our simplified coffee maker has seven design variables:

1. Capacity (max.): the maximum number of cups of coffee it can brew.

2. Capacity (min.): minimum number of cups of acceptable quality that can be brewed.

3. Footprint: area consumed on the countertop.

4. Height: height from the counter surface.

5. Max. current: maximum electrical current drawn.

6. Max. plate temp: maximum temperature the hot plate reaches (to avoid scorching the coffee or cracking the carafe).

7. Brew time (max.): brew time for maximum capacity.

As shown in Figure 9-5, we list these seven variables along the left side of the matrix and also along the top (always in the same sequence).

Figure 9-5 also indicates dependencies between the variables by placing an X in the matrix where two variables interact. For example, the second

	Capacity (max.)	Capacity (min.)	Footprint	Height	Max. current	Max. plate temp.	Brew time (max.)
Capacity (max.)	—						
Capacity (min.)	X	—					X
Footprint	X	X	—			X	
Height	X			—			
Max. current	X				—	X	X
Max. plate temp.		X	X			—	
Brew time (max.)	X			X	X		—

Figure 9-5. Design struture matrix for a coffeemaker showing calculation dependencies among seven design variables.

row (minimum capacity) has two Xs in it, indicating that in order to calculate its value, you must know two other variables, maximum capacity and brew time. Maximum capacity is no problem, because it was calculated in the previous step. But brew time represents a problem, because it will not be calculated until the last step. In a design structure matrix, any X above the diagonal (the line of minus signs) is a value that is not available yet—a problem.

Figure 9-6 is this same matrix "partitioned"—the variables have been resequenced to move as many of the Xs below the diagonal as possible and move the remaining ones into the smallest blocks possible on the diagonal. This is not a large improvement for the coffee maker, but now you can calculate two variables before encountering iteration.

	Capacity (max.)	Height	Capacity (min.)	Footprint	Max. current	Max. plate temp.	Brew time (max.)
Capacity (max.)	—						
Height	X	—					
Capacity (min.)	X		—				X
Footprint	X		X	—		X	
Max. current	X				—	X	X
Max. plate temp.			X	X		—	
Brew time (max.)	X	X			X		—

Figure 9-6. Coffeemaker design structure matrix after partitioning (resequencing the rows and columns) to minimize iteration.

As this example suggests, you are unlikely to completely eliminate iteration by simply resequencing calculations. Thus, you move to the next operation, "tearing," which means that you make an assumption about one variable above the diagonal to break (tear) a loop of iteration. We indicate the tear by changing the X to a question mark. In Figure 9-7, we have gone through two rounds of tearing to minimize the iteration.

	Capacity (max.)	Height	Brewtime (max.)	Capacity (min.)	Footprint	Max. plate temp.	Max. currenet
Capacity (max.)	—						
Height	X	—					
Brewtime (max.)	X	X	—				?
Capacity (min.)	X		X	—			
Footprint	X			X	—	?	
Max. plate temp.				X	X	—	
Max. current	X		X			X	—

Figure 9-7. Coffeemaker design structure matrix after tearing (making an assumption) where the question mark appears. The iteration loops, optimal design sequence, and required assumptions are apparent in this diagram.

Figure 9-7 lays out an optimal design process. First you specify maximum capacity, then you calculate the height. Now you have to make an assumption about the maximum current in order to proceed. Then you can calculate brew time, followed by minimum capacity. Next, you work interactively to determine footprint and maximum plate temperature by making an initial guess at the maximum plate temperature. Finally, you calculate the maximum current and then go back to check the accuracy of your initial assumed guess at this variable.

As regards risk, by partitioning you eliminate some project risk, and by isolating the tears you determine exactly where iteration will occur, so you can plan for it, although just how many loops of iteration you will need remains an uncertainty. One of the topics covered in the next chapter is tackling your highest-risk items first. DSM helps you do this because it identifies the risky areas (the assumptions) and helps you rearrange your work so that you can address them early on.

Summary

This chapter describes several tools useful for analyzing or resolving specific risks, ranging from fairly simple, general-purpose tools to more advanced ones, such as decision analysis and risk simulation, that you will probably use only occasionally for particularly important or complex risks.

The next chapter complements this one by covering some ways of thinking about risk that will be helpful throughout the risk management process.

Supplementary Reading

Eppinger, Steven D. Innovation at the speed of innovation. *Harvard Business Review* 79(1): 149–158 (January 2001). A good overview of the design structure matrix tool; it lists a URL at the end for additional information and software to perform the calculations.

Grey, Stephen. *Practical Risk Assessment for Project Management*. Chichester, UK: John Wiley & Sons, 1995. After a brief introduction, this whole book addresses risk simulation in detail, primarily using the @RISK program. It includes practical approaches for approximating probability distributions as triangles.

Schuyler, John R. *Risk and Decision Analysis in Projects*. Second edition. Newtown Square, Pennsylvania: Project Management Institute, 2001. A solid reference on decision analysis methods. The 1996 first edition also includes everything you will need to know.

10
RISK MANAGEMENT APPROACHES AND STRATEGIES

In the following sections, we describe several styles that will improve your risk management effectiveness. As you assimilate these, you may discover that they are more difficult to apply than the systematic process covered earlier because they require new attitudes and behaviors at their roots. As you read about them and start implementing them, keep in mind that, for optimal effectiveness, everyone in your organization will have to think and operate somewhat differently than before.

CAUTION

Avoid Risk When It Does Not Add Value

Although it seems too trivial to mention, many developers overlook major opportunities to avoid risk altogether—for instance, by reusing proven components and designs. For example, Hewlett-Packard encourages its engineers to reuse software because this reduces risk while saving labor. Using standard parts is a variation on this theme. Curiously, however, it is management that must encourage the reuse of designs and standard parts, because many engineers consider existing designs to be obsolete and standard parts to be inelegant solutions. If you decide to assume a risk on your project, ensure that its benefit outweighs its consequence. For instance, if you are deciding to use a nonstandard part, it should be faster, cheaper, or in some other way measurably superior to the standard part. You do not want to take on risk in the project if there is no clear competitive advantage to be gained.

KEY IDEA

Reused parts and designs do not just happen. Usually, they are planned out in earlier projects, and extra planning and design time go into them the first time around. For example, you may devote 50 percent extra design time to a part the first time it is used but then reuse it twice. This results in a 50 percent savings in design labor per design, but, more importantly for us, it means that two out of three projects will be using proven (low-risk) designs.

KEY IDEA

For reuse or standard parts to catch on, it must be easier for designers to take this route than to redesign. Provide comprehensive, easy-to-use databases of approved parts and designs to facilitate finding them. You could work this motivation issue from the other side—making it difficult to employ new parts by requiring extra paperwork and signoffs—but this is not the route to efficient product development.

Also, be careful about the signals you send to your designers. Reward those who reuse components and employ standard parts, not those who cleverly redesign a perfectly acceptable part without known economic benefit. Often, when the considerable cost of adding a new part number to inventory is taken into account, the cheaper new design will not provide a net savings.

EXAMPLE Cummins Engine Company has taken a broader approach to avoiding risk. It separated the components of its product, diesel engines, into several categories of novelty, ranging from standard parts to those few unique portions of the engine where its creativity and expertise truly makes a better engine. They handled the standard parts as above, but they dealt with the ones in the middle cleverly. These parts—for instance, the flywheel—do not contribute much distinctive value, but they must be redesigned for each engine. Consequently, Cummins automated its flywheel design by creating a "macro" that accepts a few dozen input values, which completely defines the flywheel, executes a standard set of design calculations, and outputs a set of documentation and machining files. These flywheels may not win any design awards, but they virtually eliminate design risk from these parts. Moreover, Cummins can now apply the labor saved on flywheel design to the distinctive parts of the engine, such as the head, where extra engineering effort will raise engine performance.

SCOPE In manufacturing, a common way of eliminating risk is mistake-proofing, or poka-yoke as it is known in Japan. This entails configuring parts so that they cannot be assembled incorrectly, arranging a process so that it is obvious if a step has been missed, and making similar parts in different products either identical or different enough that they cannot be confused.

Avoiding risk must be done wisely, as discussed at the end of Chapter 1. This is not an excuse to be risk averse and shun all risk, as this will drive out the very innovation you seek. The trick is to constantly consider risk in light of the value it could bring to your project. Avoid taking on risk when it does not add value commensurate with its cost. Exploit it when its likely benefit exceeds its cost.

You may recall that we covered avoidance in Chapter 7 as a type of risk action plan. There is a connection between avoidance as described there and the type discussed here. Both are connected with the decisions you make. In Chapter 7, we discovered avoidance plans by revisiting tacit decisions that unknowingly introduced risk when they were made, and then we built avoidance plans by reversing these decisions. Here, we suggest that you become more mindful of such decisions so that you can make them more explicitly. In so doing, you align your decisions with your risk strategy in advance, rather than having to reverse decisions later through a risk action plan. Clearly, the approach taken here is more proactive.

Stay Flexible on Unresolved Issues

If you can narrow a risk down to just two possible solutions, sometimes you can keep both solutions open. For example, Black & Decker con- EXAMPLE
ducted focus groups on handle size and shape for a battery-powered screwdriver. It knew this was a critical choice, but it was unable to decide between two options: a slim one—more comfortable for smaller hands, but holding only two cells—and a somewhat fatter handle holding three cells for greater power. Unsure about the handle, Black & Decker decided to build *both* sets of handle tooling and actually start production with one while doing more market research.

After several years of offering various mouse alternatives, such as track- EXAMPLE
balls, on notebook computers, manufacturers seem to be settling on either a stylus or a touchpad. On some Dell notebooks, the developers offer both devices rather than risk a poor choice. Even though this increases product cost, it is insignificant relative to the lost profits incurred if a wrong choice is implemented.

In R&D, this approach is called parallel design effort; in Chapter 7, we call it redundancy. A second group designs an alternative part that is less risky but also perhaps more expensive or of lower performance. They continue on this backup design until it is clear that the primary design will succeed, then they abandon the backup. Sometimes, as with the Black & Decker handles, the backup design actually moves into production until a better alternative becomes apparent. Notice that Dell seems to be pursuing its stylus redundancy indefinitely.

Clearly, you cannot afford to use this rather expensive option on too many uncertainties!

SCOPE You can use a similar approach in manufacturing. One company foresaw that they would need higher-precision machining capabilities for a new generation of products soon, so before they actually needed that precision, they bought and installed the new machines. Then they learned the capabilities of the new machining process on existing parts, initially forfeiting unneeded precision, then moving toward it on the new-generation products only when they were sure of it.

Chapter 7 describes how you can employ redundancy in your risk management process by formulating redundancy plans.

Maintain Contact with Customers

Perhaps the best general-purpose means of reducing market risk is to put your design engineers in direct contact with customers and user situations.
EXAMPLE Black & Decker gets its designers into the field by sending them out to ride with technicians in the firm's DeWALT® vans as the technicians make their rounds of construction sites and home centers. Boeing, when developing its 777 airliner, asked its customer, United Airlines, to send several United operations experts to join the development team at Boeing. It gave
EXAMPLE these customers unrestricted freedom to review documents and attend meetings as they mingled with the developers. A telecommunications equipment provider, Tellabs, has its engineers test their products jointly with customers during the integration phase. This is done before the product is released so the development team can gain insight into the operational aspects and make any necessary changes to support the customer once the product is deployed.

EXAMPLE A start-up surgical instrument company in Silicon Valley lacked the funds to hire a surgeon to work with it to design its product, so the engineers devised a bold solution. They found out where surgeons congregate before performing operations at Stanford University Hospital, then used the surgeons' idle time to get "complimentary" customer input on their designs.

In other situations where direct access to customers is difficult to achieve, you can perhaps involve some of your own people who have extensive contact with customers, such as field service or customer service staff. For example, Invetech, an Australian contract biomedical instrument developer, lacks such personnel (because their products are developed for clients), so they take this approach one step further. Invetech involves field service personnel from client organizations throughout each development project—including early reviews, hands-on exposure to design concepts, and assisting with prototype builds.

We could give many other similar examples, but with a little creativity you will find some that fit your business and markets better. Just remember that to gain the greatest value from customer contact, design engineers must be in direct contact with customers, not just interacting through intermediaries, such as marketing. Also, arrange this contact to occur proactively before design decisions are made. All too often, engineers visit customers to fix problems during field trials, after the problems have been designed into the product!

KEY IDEA

Customer contact and most other customer research techniques work best for established products, where customers can respond to the actual experience of using the product. When you are working in a cutting-edge field, you have to be highly creative in finding actual usage experience. For example, when developing radically new surgical infection-control techniques (for humans), 3M used a so-called lead user method to gain experience from veterinarians, who practice in a more innovative, less-regulated market.

EXAMPLE

Also, be sure to keep in regular contact with key customers during development. They change their minds and you change your designs, so new risks are likely to arise as old ones are resolved. Customer-related risks that arise while the project is under way are often called scope creep (see "Identifying New Risks" in Chapter 8 for details). Whether such risks are genuinely new, or simply reflect that your initial customer research or risk identification was weak, the result is the same—a newly identified risk to the project. A regular process to monitor the customer environment is your best defense against scope-creep risks.

Address the Risky Items First

When faced with an assortment of tasks, as is the case in a development project, the natural human tendency is to start with the easiest. This gives people a sense of confidence that fortifies them to tackle the tougher parts. Although there may be a great deal of wisdom to this bootstrapping strategy in general, it is exactly the wrong way to approach a product development project. If you cannot handle the difficult, high-risk items, cancel the project before you put any effort into the easy ones! Even if you are successful ultimately, it is the difficult, high-risk tasks that are likely to have the greatest impact on your critical path. Thus, they should be undertaken first, and their risk resolved early on. Addressing riskier items first is one way of being proactive about risk management.

EXAMPLE Many product developers call this a fail-fast strategy. Here is an example of how MDS Sciex, a Canadian manufacturer of analytical instruments, managed risk by failing fast while developing their QSTAR quadruple time-of-flight instrument. The projected size and weight of QSTAR was two to three times greater than any of their current instruments. The project's risk identification exposed the possibility of failing shock and vibration tests under shipping conditions. Consequently, the team accelerated development of the instrument's frame and shipping crate and engaged a finite-element analysis consultant to discover potential weak areas in the frame and crate. To validate the finite-element analysis, they built a breadboard frame and shipping crate using wooden structures and weights to simulate the heavy components, as the actual components were not available yet. This exercise allowed them to modify their design before building prototype instruments. This prevention plan was successful in mitigating risk because the prototype instrument passed subsequent testing.

This example is especially interesting because it runs counter to normal practice in two ways. Normally, the frame is the last part that would be released from design, as everything else attaches to it, so it is subject to continuing revision. MDS Sciex totally reversed this sequence. Second, in our experience, the crate or other packaging often falls into the "cracks" between departments because it is not the clear responsibility of any one department. Thus, it becomes a catch-up item when it is discovered. The team also reversed this sequence.

Modern software development has moved naturally toward resolving high-risk items first. Software development now employs object-oriented programming, a technique that facilitates iterative development. In each of several preplanned loops of iteration, developers produce a functional program, which becomes more robust and gains more features in later iterations. In planning the content of each iterative loop, it is good practice to put high-risk items in the early loops. The reason is the same one we stated before: if the project is a no-go, you are better off terminating it early, and even if it proceeds, resolving the high-risk items will make the whole project more predictable.

SCOPE

The design structure matrix tool (discussed in Chapter 9) also helps you address riskier items first. It helps you understand and manage the major assumptions you will have to make—which are the high-risk items—in any process, so that you can move them to the beginning of the project, just as object-oriented programmers do with their identified risks.

Like many of these approaches, this is really a mindset that must be assimilated by everyone on your team—indeed, by your whole organization—in order to be effective. Everyone should be aware of the high-risk items and push them to the top of their priority lists. If this counterintuitive behavior is not developed explicitly, the natural tendency will be to let difficult items slide.

In this connection, watch your project metrics. Often, metrics count the number of tasks completed by a certain time. Although this metric has the great benefit of avoiding partial credit for task completion and the fudging that it encourages, it does encourage developers to complete the easy tasks first to make their metrics look good—the opposite of what good risk management requires.

CAUTION

Even if you do not have such a metric, be careful how you reward progress on a project. This is just one example of how difficult it is to build reward systems that encourage the behavior you desire (for more on the difficulties of creating reward systems, see Kohn in "Supplementary Reading" in Chapter 11).

Apportion Risk Carefully

Along with getting a jump-start on high-risk areas, be careful about how you apportion risk in the product. It is best to concentrate risk in a few known areas where you can watch it very carefully (as the example in the following paragraph will illustrate). If you don't, you can easily end up in a situation where moderate risks distributed throughout the design accumulate toward a high overall threat to the project. After you concentrate your risks, assign some of your best developers to these areas, and emphasize to management that these risks warrant extra attention. You might also engage a technical consultant with the specific expertise needed or assign someone who is normally a manager but has the particular skill you need.

Figure 10-1 provides a numerical example of this phenomenon. It assumes that the product has 10 modules, each of which is necessary for the product to function. In the first line of the figure, we distribute risk by using a new technology, with 90 percent chance of working, in each module. The overall chance of success for the project is only 35 percent. In the second line, we concentrate risk by keeping existing technologies in all but the 10th module, raising their success probabilities to 99 percent and thus the overall project success rate to a dramatically higher 82 percent. The third line shows that we could even use a questionable new technology with an 80 percent success probability in our high-risk module and still maintain a much better project success probability than with distributed risk.

EXAMPLE Consider how MDS Sciex applied this principle while developing their API 3000 mass spectrometer. This team concentrated its development efforts on only two critical subsystems (the high vacuum subsystem and the ion path subsystem) that provided significant improvements in performance to the customer. By concentrating on two subsystems and using existing subsystems from the predecessor, model API 365, they avoided additional integration risks in the API 3000. Subsequently, they used the same approach on their API 4000, which replaced the API 3000. In this project, MDS Sciex concentrated performance enhancements in only three subsystems: the ion sources, the user interface, and the gas supplies. The latter two subsystems were of lower risk, since they were extensions of existing technology. This allowed them to concentrate risk management attention

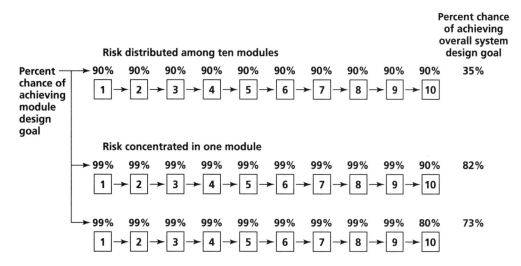

Figure 10-1. By concentrating system risk in one module (second line), the chance of overall system success is much higher than it is in the case of uniformly distributed risk (first line).

on development of the new ion sources. The combined performance improvements of the two products have allowed MDS Sciex's customers to detect substances undetectable with the API 365 and detectible with difficulty with the API 3000, and they achieved this through changes in only five subsystems.

Returning to the subject of management attention: an excellent way to foster it is through "management by walking around" (MBWA). MBWA, coined by the founders of Hewlett Packard over 50 years ago, is especially beneficial in high-risk areas of fast-moving projects because it gives management unfiltered, real-time information on progress and problems. Importantly, it also allows dialog and problem solving when needed, rather than misjudging or waiting until problems get out of hand. In companies where this culture is established, MBWA is practiced by all managers from first-level supervisors to the CEO; in others, it is practiced sporadically only by those who appreciate its value.

In reference to both Figure 10-1 and MBWA, remember that the risk in a system often resides in the interfaces between modules. Therefore, do not take Figure 10-1 to mean that the modules should be your only focus. You can use techniques such as MBWA to monitor these sensitive areas, and you can also ensure that designers on both sides of an interface communicate regularly. Finally, you can avoid some interface risk by using industry-standard interfaces wherever possible, just as you would use standard parts to avoid risk.

Test at a Low Level

We often resolve technical risk through some kind of testing. Testing applies to nontechnical areas as well—for instance, employing a focus group to resolve market risk. Even functions such as purchasing can resolve risks through testing, by having a supplier build a part using a new process solely to test that process before it is on the project's critical path, for instance.

To focus your testing, and to make it proactive, test at the lowest level possible. Testing components and subsystems before you complete a product gives you quick answers to specific questions. These specific questions should stem from your risk action plans (see Chapter 7).

EX**A**MPLE This concept of testing at a low level is precisely what allowed the Wright brothers to beat their competition to market with the first flyable aircraft in 1903. Whereas competitors tried to make progress most logically—by designing, building, and flying a complete aircraft to test their theories— the Wright brothers observed instead that several areas of risk had to be resolved first. These included the techniques of lift, propulsion, and control. Consequently, they tested simple components and subsystems to resolve risks quickly at this level first. For example, they tested sections of propellers in a wind tunnel before they even bothered to build a complete propeller. They could build and test propeller sections faster than complete propellers, and far faster than complete airplanes.

CAUTION However, when following this approach, you should also keep in mind a shortcoming of resolving risk at a subsystem or component level: the complete system still may not work when integrated. Consequently, you must anticipate and plan for such integration risks. Integration risks are becoming increasingly prevalent as systems become more complex, and as low-level testing delays their discovery. You can use various approaches to avoid integration risk, such as employing interfaces between modules that isolate the effects of one module on another.

As with many of the other approaches in this chapter, testing at a low level is a discipline that is most effective when assimilated throughout the organization. The philosophy behind low-level testing is that each test is a verification/refutation of a hypothesis. To effectively focus your testing, explicitly establish the hypothesis first, and then design a test solely to resolve this question. If you need to check two hypotheses, consider using two simpler tests. In this way testing becomes more focused, and thus proactive.

KEY IDEA

To effectively test at a low level, make sure that you have an infrastructure that supports it. Minimize the paperwork and approvals needed to run simple tests, make model shops and test facilities readily available to designers, and pre-establish accounts with local contractors who can get simple work done easily and quickly.

Use Failure to Your Advantage

Risk management has to do with reducing the possibility of suffering a loss, that is, of failing. Interestingly, however, failures provide valuable information that helps us to develop products faster. Thus, failures are not always to be avoided.

Step back and think of product development as a learning process. We learn the most from an experiment or test when we have no idea beforehand how it will turn out. Ironically, if we design an experiment so that we expect it to be successful, and it is in fact successful, then we have learned nothing. To accelerate learning, design your experiments so that the expectation beforehand lies midway between passing and failing, as suggested in Figure 10-2. Then the outcome provides the greatest information and allows you to progress rapidly.

For example, a firm that makes commercial door locks, which must pass a severe and expensive fire test conducted by an independent laboratory, customarily designed its locks conservatively, so that they would always pass the test, due to the high cost of the test. However, this company found that it could resolve risk earlier by designing the locks quickly, with only partial confidence that they would pass the test. Then it used the initial test results to learn where the lock needed more strength. Not only did this raise the odds of passing the final test, but it also meant that they were not adding

EXAMPLE

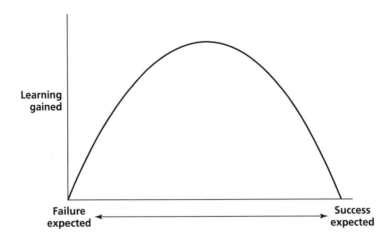

Figure 10-2. Learning from an experiment depends on what you expect to happen beforehand, so to learn the most, plan experiments to occur midway between where you would expect success and where failure is expected.

extra metal (extra cost) to the lock as a safety margin, nor were they wasting design labor on items providing no competitive advantage.

There is an exception to designing tests and experiments for learning, however. Some tests are not intended for learning but instead for verification that you have a commercially acceptable design. Such tests often come at the end of development, where they can involve lengthy life testing for millions of cycles. Should the product fail such a test, you face a big surprise and enormous schedule disruption. The appropriate time for learning is at the beginning of the project, not the end.

KEY IDEA

Consequently, consider the purpose of each test or experiment before undertaking it. If it is intended for learning—as many will be, especially if you are operating in a proactive mode—design the test so that the outcome is as uncertain as possible to maximize the rate of learning. However, if you want to verify that your design meets specifications, arrange your prior learning to make passing the final test as certain as possible. In fact, if it is a lengthy test and you have high confidence of passing, you may be able to take the test off your critical path. For example, you could start production while you complete the final life test, accumulating some inventory to accelerate market launch.

The award-winning product development firm, IDEO, institutionalizes the early-failure mindset through their motto, "Fail often to succeed sooner." However, this does not mean, at IDEO or elsewhere, shoddy thinking or lack of professional judgment—an important distinction. Harvard Business School professor Stefan Thomke makes this clearer: "Fail early and often, but avoid mistakes." By mistakes, he means poorly designed experiments, lack of a hypothesis guiding an experiment, or poor control over extraneous variables that could cloud the results.

In most companies, purposely designing experiments that might fail goes against the success-driven culture of "doing it right the first time." Consequently, in order to keep your job while "designing for failure," your strategy of early, small failures must be communicated to and accepted by everyone up to the CEO level.

CAUTION

Summary

It is comforting to think of risk management as a process with certain steps to be checked off. But underlying effective risk management, regardless of the process used, are certain ways of thinking and operating. Working on the high-risk items first, planning to fail, and related behaviors may not be easy to acquire, but they distinguish outstanding risk managers from average ones.

The next chapter moves further into these behavioral and organizational issues to help you implement an effective, enduring risk management program in your company.

Supplementary Reading

Reinertsen, Donald G. *Managing the Design Factory*. New York: The Free Press, 1997. Reinertsen offers an excellent conceptual treatment of exploiting failure, based on information theory (Chapter 4).

Smith, Preston G. and Reinertsen, Donald G. *Developing Products in Half the Time*. New York: John Wiley & Sons, 1998. Chapter 12 of this book covers the risk management approaches discussed in our current Chapter 10 plus some related ones. Chapter 6 provides more detail on apportioning risk.

11

IMPLEMENTING A PROJECT RISK MANAGEMENT PROGRAM SUCCESSFULLY

Until now, we have concentrated on applying project risk management to a single project. The presumption with most such techniques seems to be that if you apply them to one project, they will spread naturally to others. This presumption leads to the phenomenon known as "management fad of the month": introducing a new improvement program regularly and expecting that it will instantaneously become established.

This does *not* happen, and presuming otherwise simply frustrates management and leads to cynicism among workers. We suggest that unless you intend to make project risk management a way of life in your organization, then you are wasting your time by even starting down this path—and the same applies to any other business improvement program you may be considering. It is perfectly acceptable to implement a scaled-down version of project risk management, perhaps applying it only to major projects, only to breakthrough projects, or by monitoring risk only at project phase reviews rather than at weekly team meetings. You can start with a small-scale version and add to it as you demonstrate success, which is Shaffer's approach (see "Supplementary Reading"). But to achieve ongoing success, you must work diligently at establishing the program at whatever scale you decide to implement.

KEY IDEA

The reason for this is simple. Project risk management, at its roots, requires changes in the ways that team members, team leaders, and management behave, and changes in behavior, although quite possible, are not automatic. Here, to reiterate, are some of the changes in behavior that may be required:

- being proactive in identifying and resolving project risks;
- operating cross-functionally (although most companies now have what they call cross-functional teams, these are often what product development guru Robert Cooper calls "fake teams"—see "Supplementary Reading");

- overcoming the firefighting style of some managers;
- being willing to invest time and money proactively in risks *before* they become issues;
- moving beyond a tendency toward pessimism by team members, under which identifying a long list of project risks can only reinforce their pessimism; and
- avoiding an aversion to paperwork and "regimentation" that is often resisted by engineers and other creative types.

Clearly, these are serious issues, but fortunately, there are effective means of dealing with them. This chapter will help you truly establish project risk management as a natural activity in your organization, but doing so will require diligent effort on your behalf. Consequently, this is perhaps the most important chapter in the book for those who are serious about making project risk management a way of life in their organizations.

Based on our experience in implementing project risk management and similar initiatives in many other product development organizations, we provide here our suggestions on the critical points to keep in mind as you implement project risk management in your organization. In many cases, we review, reframe, or reinforce material covered in other chapters. Thus, although this is not an overview of the risk management process, it is a summary of the book from a program implementation viewpoint.

Fitting Risk Management into Project Management

Over the past several years, project risk management has been recognized as being integral to effective project management. For instance, it is now one of nine areas of knowledge in the Project Management Institute's body of knowledge, along with the management of scope, cost, and schedule (see "Supplementary Reading" for Chapter 1). We treat risk management separately only because we have found that it fails to receive the attention it deserves when consolidated with mainstream project management—that is, with activities such as schedule and budget management. However, effective risk management should not be altogether foreign to project managers, seeing as it involves familiar activities such as creating risk action plans and monitoring and reporting on identified risks.

Because the early risk management activities interact with other early pro-ject activities, there is no completely clean way to fit risk management into other activities. From a project perspective, risk planning is just another facet in planning the project during its front end. After experi-menting with various places to insert risk planning, we have developed the process flow illustrated in Figure 11-1. To make risk management an integral part of your project management methodology, you must design a process clearly establishing the expectation that proactive management of your risks is the norm. Figure 11-1 outlines a typical product development process to illustrate how its front end can be designed to support risk management. (This process illustrated here is for developing a piece of capital equipment, so your process probably will look somewhat different.)

KEY IDEA

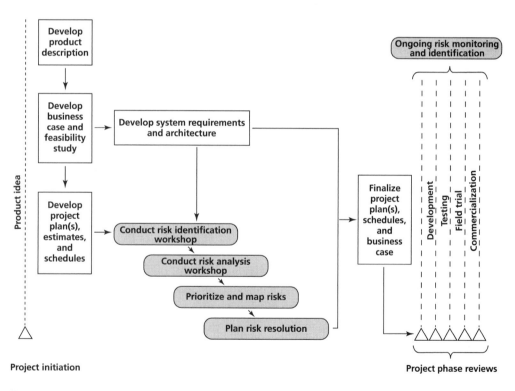

Figure 11-1. This simplified product development process, emphasizing the front end, illustrates how risk management can be integrated into a product development methodology.

We would like to begin risk management even earlier, but we have found that you will need certain critical information before you engage an entire product development team to pursue your project's risks. Consequently, go ahead and develop initial project plans and schedules to be used for initiating risk identification workshops. When we tried to conduct risk identification prior to this step, we found ourselves formulating generic and imaginary risks because we did not understand the project well enough in terms of scope, budget, schedule, and resources. In addition, you may find that some iteration is needed due to other information, such as system requirements, appearing after you complete the initial workshops.

The risk workshops will more than likely change your initial project assumptions, dependencies, and constraints. Therefore, revise your project plans, schedules, and business case before you close the front end.

BUILD RISK MANAGEMENT INTO ALL PROJECT PHASES

If there is a single key to making project risk management "stick" in your organization, it is to make it an integral part of all project phases and treat it just as seriously as you do project scope, budgeting, scheduling, and resource allocation. As a seasoned project manager, you may recognize that of these four items, resources are critical for making progress. You may have the best schedule imaginable, but without resources to support it your schedule is fiction.

Consequently, always consider the resource implications of managing project risk. Resources include time, money, and people. If you need to draw in experts from outside of the project to identify and analyze risks, arrange whatever it takes to assure their genuine participation. When you create risk action plans, provide for the resources necessary to support them. This is especially true if you suspect that you will need substantial resources. In extreme cases, the resources needed to manage a single crucial risk that you have discovered could be so great as to make the project financially infeasible. Proactive risk management demands that you cancel the project or greatly restructure it in response to such information. In short, you are practicing poor project management if you assume that you can just squeeze such substantial additional effort out of your assigned resources.

Project risk management has many benefits, and it also has clear costs. Your job, as project manager, is to ascertain that the benefits outweigh the costs. But you will fail if you attempt to balance this equation by ignoring the resources your program will expend.

The simplest means of building risk management into your project is to ensure that the early steps—identification, analysis, prioritizing and mapping, and risk resolution planning—are a normal part of an early project phase. Then, establish risk monitoring as a normal, regular part of your other project monitoring activities. For example, if you have a formal action-item tracking system, then you should track risk items as well. Finally, each risk under management should be listed as a separate project task, including its assigned resources, responsible individual, deliverables, and due date.

PROVIDE DATA MANAGEMENT TOOLS

Project risk management entails tracking a substantial amount of data as you move through the five steps of the process. You may identify 100 risks initially, and some of the important ones will involve many plans that need monitoring. To make implementation easy and attractive to your teams, and to provide a consistent format to simplify comparison across projects, develop some uniform data management tools. The "Spreadsheets" section in Chapter 9 describes some of these, and others appear in Chapters 4 through 8 covering steps of the process.

These tools are not complicated, and they can take many forms. We suggest that you start with spreadsheets. The first team to use project risk management can create these. If you want to jump-start the process, assign a spreadsheet expert to work with the first team to build their forms as they go through the five steps. As these spreadsheets become polished and reasonably stable templates, you might consider converting them to web-based versions or building them into your enterprise data management or product development data management system.

These data management activities also help institutionalize your risk management process by standardizing data presentation format and nomenclature. Thus, if a team is not doing risk management adequately, this is more likely to be apparent.

Implementation Guidance

Following are nine topics that we have found critical to successful implementation. In many cases, they cover concepts also described in earlier chapters. For example, we first discussed risk as an opportunity in the "Risk As an Ally" section of Chapter 1 because it is an essential concept in understanding how to view risk in a project. We also address it here because, if you implement risk management without considering the positive side of risk, you are likely to create a bureaucratic, risk-averse implementation.

Consequently, rather than merely considering this an overview of risk management, please ponder as you read on: "What am I going to do to make this program stick in *my* organization?" In doing so, should you find something that seems quite foreign to your corporate culture, you have likely uncovered a potentially serious implementation hurdle—a program implementation risk that you have identified proactively, as it were.

CONSIDER RISK ALSO AS AN OPPORTUNITY

As we suggested in Chapter 1, think of risk as both a potential for loss and an opportunity for gain. We have emphasized the loss aspect, because our goal is to eliminate the surprises that go with such losses. However, there is a more optimistic view, because once you understand and quantify risks, they can be your allies. For example, consider the risk of committing to a piece of tooling, such as a mold, before you have all of the information necessary to build it. Comfortable risk-avoidance practice would suggest waiting until this information is available, but waiting could delay the project by a month. Alternatively, by understanding and quantifying the risk involved, you can decide how you wish to deal with it. Consider the decision tree in Figure 11-2 (see Chapter 9 for more on decision trees). If the tool fails due to your incomplete information, which you estimate will happen 25 percent of the time, you lose an average of SF12,500 (Swiss francs). However, if the cost of delay for the project (see Smith and Reinertsen in "Supplementary Reading" for Chapter 7) is SF500,000 per month, you stand to gain SF375,000 on average. Thus, on average, you are ahead SF362,500 net every time you take this risk, even though you stand to lose SF50,000 every time. The company that does not understand the opportunity side of risk will issue a policy prohibiting

EXAMPLE

the procurement of tooling speculatively the first time they lose SF50,000, thus closing the door to this lucrative strategy and many others like it.

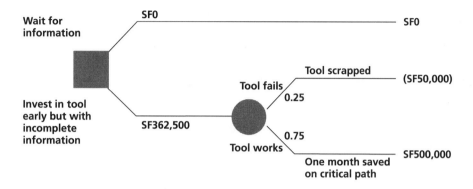

Figure 11-2. Decision tree showing that by using partial information (at the risk of being wrong) to invest in tooling early, one month, SF500,000, can be saved, which is worth SF362,500, on average, to the project.

This material is used by permission of John Wiley & Sons, Inc. Adapted from Preston G. Smith and Donald G. Reinertsen, *Developing Products in Half the Time*, ©1998 Preston G. Smith and Donald G. Reinertsen.

TRAIN YOUR PEOPLE

Each person has his or her own notion of risk. Without training, individuals will argue about what is really a risk, will have no means of determining a risk's likelihood or total loss, and will fail at creating actionable risk resolution plans. To appreciate how pervasive adequate training is in the risk management process, see the listings under *training* in the index. In this book, we have been careful to define and use terms consistently, provide a glossary, and offer a risk model to act as a common framework for addressing risk. For your team to manage risk effectively, each member must understand these terms and concepts and gain some hands-on practice in applying them. Especially for your first projects, have someone experienced with the techniques readily available to coach the teams after the initial training.

Training also extends to management. As we have warned before, if management is not trained in the basic concepts and terminology, your team will suffer through chaotic management reviews while managers argue about the process and attempt to redefine the terms you are using. Management's training can be considerably briefer than the team's training, but it must also encompass different topics, as described in the Introduction.

Just who conducts this training depends on where the expertise resides. It might be in human resources, a corporate university, or a group of project managers who have received outside training. If there is no one qualified internally to conduct the training, you should engage an outside trainer to get started.

MAKE RISK A CONCERN OF MANAGEMENT

As you proceed, integrate your managers, at all levels, into institutional-ization of the risk management process (Chapters 4 through 8) and behaviors (Chapter 10). Chapter 3 of this book provides an "executive summary," but we have found that you cannot depend on management absorbing this material by simply reading one chapter in a book. Man-agement should receive live overview training—for example, in inter-preting a top 10 list, a risk map, or your risk dashboard—so that they appreciate risk management and its benefits. If this does not happen, two outcomes are likely:

CAUTION

- Management will inadvertently undermine the program; for exam-ple, by reassigning an individual who is working a critical risk action plan.
- Through lack of apparent management interest (for instance, if managers do not ask risk management questions at phase review meetings), team members will infer that management does not really care about managing risks, and the program will wither gradually.

Here again, let the schedule and the budget be your touchstones: if man-agement exhibits a lack of interest in a critical risk that they express in a schedule or budget item, your program may be in jeopardy.

TAKE POTENTIAL PROBLEMS SERIOUSLY

Many managers have difficulty spending money or other resources on prob-lems that might not materialize. They have to deal with enough problems that are already active. Although these managers will readily buy fire insur-ance on the building, they are reluctant to invest in potential problems until their existence is clear. Unfortunately, this reactive approach usually leads to fewer and more expensive risk-resolution solutions and is far more disruptive to the schedule. Not taking potential problems seriously is similar to the firefighting behavior described in Chapter 1, but in this case it is more of a financial aversion to insuring for events that may not happen, rather than the type of excitement and instant gratification that feeds firefighting.

This is a crucial point because, until you can take *potential* problems seriously, you will not achieve *proactive* risk management.

CAUTION

There are two steps in dealing with this phenomenon. First, observe that some of yesterday's potential problems are today's actual problems, so management is consumed with actual problems today because they did not avert them yesterday. That is, being overloaded with current problems is a self-fulfilling prophecy.

Second, to clarify the value of acting in advance on potential problems, analyze what some past problems would have cost had they been dealt with before they occurred. Most likely, your analysis will show that addressing problems proactively is considerably cheaper than dealing with them reactively, even taking into account that not all potential risks will happen. (If your analysis does not show this, then either you have many risks with low risk likelihoods or you are not addressing risks with high risk-reduction leverage, as discussed in Chapter 7.)

SPARE THE MESSENGER

For various reasons, some organizations develop a culture that shuns bad news—into which category, unfortunately, risk falls. The most apparent version of this is the "kill the messenger" syndrome. Milder forms include people who do not want to "look bad" in front of management or want to be "team players." In some cultures, individuals do not want to stand out or "rock the boat." Conversely, in individualistic cultures, teams and managers want to appear in total control and able to handle anything that arises; discussing risks does not fit with this stance.

Effective risk management requires a certain level of honesty about how things really are. If team members perceive that it is not safe to be open or proactive about project risks, all your sources of proactive risk

KEY IDEA

management will dry up. This does not mean that the whole team should have a negative prognosis for the project, but it does mean that it must be possible to bring up risk candidates freely and analyze them openly to determine if they merit attention. (See the section, "Balance Between Optimism and Pessimism," in Chapter 4 for more on this topic.)

Observe that if you handle your risk communications well, you can turn bad news into good news, not only by presenting the risks but, more importantly, what you are doing about them. By showing executive management your progress regarding risk action plans, you can establish a sense of control, even when your project is facing substantial risk.

DO NOT LET THE ENGINEERS RUN PROJECT RISK MANAGEMENT

CAUTION

A theme that should be clear by now is that good risk management is cross-functional. If engineers dominate product development, you might consider letting engineering run project risk management. This is a mistake. If you assign risk management to the engineering department and engage only engineers to identify, analyze, and plan for risks, they will place only engineering risks on their lists.

If you have forgotten it, turn back to the postage meter example at the beginning of Chapter 1 to observe how few project risks actually are likely to be engineering related. Engineers already have a means of managing technical risks—failure mode and effects analysis (FMEA). This process deals with engineering risks well, but it is not project risk management (see Chapter 1 for further discussion of FMEA).

Many organizations have faced this issue regarding project management in general; that is, if they place project management under engineering, they will not have truly cross-functional product development. They have found various creative solutions for making project management cross-functional in their organizations, depending on their culture and organizational structure. In view of this, we cannot give you specific instructions on where to place project risk management, but we do know that it cannot be solely an engineering activity and it should not even be an engineering-centric one.

COLLECT AND PUBLICIZE RISK METRICS

Earlier, in the section entitled "Take Potential Problems Seriously," we cautioned that management, especially executive and financial management, can be reluctant to spend time or money on potential problems, given that there seem to be plenty of actual ones. This stance is incompatible with effective project risk management because it precludes being proactive about risk.

Risk management metrics are your defense against this attitude. Using strategic metrics (see Chapter 8), you should be able to show how many risks were averted and how much time or money this saved the organization. Although you will have to proceed on faith initially, when you have no metrics to justify resolving risks proactively, over time your strategic metrics can build solid justification for being proactive about risk management.

Recall what we said about strategic metrics in Chapter 8. First, they should remain stable in what they measure so that you can see long-term trends. Second, you should start collecting them before you start managing project risks, so that they can illustrate the effect on performance should your risk management program be terminated. Third, metrics—strategic or tactical—are only useful if they are shared with employees. Especially in the case of something as "potential" as risks, publicize your strategic metrics to demonstrate the ongoing value of your project risk management program.

JUMP IN

These techniques will do you no good unless you try them out, and the best time to do this is now, while they are fresh in your mind.

KEY IDEA

The fastest, most effective way to get started is to designate a pilot project. Consider this a special project, and train only those people who will be involved in it. Keep track of what works for you, what needs bolstering, and what can be eliminated or cut back as you work through this project. Then develop a rollout plan to institutionalize the process by documenting it and training participants in other projects.

CAUTION

A word of warning: we have seen many pilot projects succeed wonderfully, followed by second-generation projects that failed. A pilot strategy is a great way to move quickly and at low risk, but your initiative will continue to need special care through a few generations before it succeeds and becomes established. Be especially careful about expanding the program at a rate higher than you can support adequately with trained people. Consciously develop a cadre of risk management experts who can train and coach others in the process. The icons in the margins of this book alert you to many pitfalls, and these will take on real immediacy as your people experience them. At such times risk management experts are valuable to propagating the program.

DO NOT OVERSELL PROJECT RISK MANAGEMENT

CAUTION

A project risk management program can make substantial improvements in your projects' predictability. But it should be clear by now that it is not a cure-all. First, you will expend a significant amount of effort to implement project risk management. And each project will take additional effort, although this should be more than offset by the time and money saved from averted risks.

You have also learned that project risk management is not a blissful existence of "no surprises," only one of reduced surprises. You cannot afford to liminate all risks that you know about, and others are simply unknowable. Risk management is a constant game of improving your odds.

Continuously Improve Your Implementation

We wish that we could provide you with exactly the project risk management implementation that will be best for you. In reality, every organization will need a different implementation strategy to meet its needs well, and even these needs will change over time. We have tried to both suggest a middle-of-the-road means of implementation and provide some alternatives for you to use in adapting the process. For example, we provide several ways of identifying risks, several models to use in analyzing them, and a few means of prioritizing your results.

You will find the implementation that works for you only by experiment-ing. This is why it is essential to think of your project risk management program as an evolving one, to keep track of what is working and what is not quite right yet, and to make adjustments accordingly.

KEY IDEA

Put another way, project risk management requires a considerable invest-ment and provides considerable benefits. You gain the greatest value by adjusting the process to achieve the best outcome for the effort expended. Your objective should be to make your process as "lean" as possible, elimi-nating portions that do not contribute value commensurate with the effort required. Here we offer a means for doing this by continually reassessing your effectiveness.

EXTRACT THE LEARNING FROM EACH PROJECT

Each product development project offers two deliverables. The obvious one is the new product that you ship. The other deliverable is learning about how well you conducted this project—in this case, learning about your risk management performance. You forfeit the second deliverable unless you are quite clear upfront about expecting it.

KEY IDEA

Usually, you acquire this learning by conducting a post-project review (the common name for such a review is post mortem, but we avoid this term, which suggests that something has died). The process is much like the risk identification step: assemble a diverse project team, with a facilitator if possible, and use cues, such as your product development process map (see Figure 4-2) or a prompt list, to elicit observations on what was or was not especially effective or time-consuming. You are looking for four types of situations:

- items that could be added to your risk management process to make it work better,
- items that you could remove from the process without much loss of effectiveness,
- modifications you could make to parts of your risk management process to render them more effective, or
- changes that you could make in how you develop new products that would avoid certain risks that you experienced in this project.

This last item is especially powerful because it represents an enduring improvement in how you develop products and a reduction in your risk management effort. For example, consider Gem City Engineering (GCE), a Dayton, Ohio, USA, manufacturer of small batches of highly specialized machines for the semiconductor and related industries.

EXAMPLE

Due to the nature of their business and their customer contracts, engineering changes and their resulting costs have always been project risk items. Consequently, GCE created a detailed Change Record Sheet (CRS) spreadsheet that it requires for every project. The project manager can then track the time and money associated with each change by department, and knows upfront whether GCE or the customer will be paying for the change. The CRS, unique to GCE's situation, has averted countless risks that would have otherwise arisen.

As you consider how to conduct post-project reviews, keep these points in mind:

- Work from your metrics, to tell you whether the items you are considering improving are significant or frequent enough to be worthy of your attention.

- Do not consider this an audit. An audit compares what happened with what the process said should happen—did you follow the rules? In this case, you are considering whether the rules themselves might need to be changed.

- Be careful about combining this risk-management learning session with other wrap-up meetings that you might conduct at the end of the project, such as a financial or market review. These other objectives are valuable in themselves but powerful enough to destroy your learning objective (see Smith and Reinertsen in "Supplementary Reading" for details).

- Your only goal is *actual* improvements in how you conduct risk management, or improvements in your development process to preclude risks. A goal of delivering a report gets you less than halfway there. Even implementation plans are fiction unless accompanied by sufficient resources to execute them, as you learned in Chapter 7.

As you improve your risk management process, keep it flexible. Small projects may be ideally suited for light-duty risk management approaches that you have found inadequate for large, high-stakes projects.

Summary

Relative to conducting a successful program on one project, successfully implementing an enduring risk management program in an organization requires a broader view and one more sensitive to organizational dynamics and politics. The critical step is to build risk management in as an integral part of all project phases. You will know that you have succeeded when risk management becomes as important as the budget or the schedule. This chapter has covered several factors that will help risk management thrive in your organization, such as training managers, being open to bad news, and not letting the engineers run the program. Finally, we explained how to adapt the program continuously to your unique, evolving needs.

Supplementary Reading

Cooper, Robert G. *Winning at New Products*, Third Edition. Cambridge, Massachusetts: Perseus Books, 2001. Although most organizations today claim to already have cross-functional teams, Cooper calls many of them "fake" or "pretend" teams that are clearly subservient to the functional organization and thus have little power to take action; he lists the earmarks of such teams (p. 119).

Kohn, Alfie. *Punished by Rewards*. Boston: Houghton Mifflin, 1993. When implementing programs such as risk management, implementers often consider various rewards to encourage compliance. Read Kohn's sobering view before you take this approach.

Shaffer, Robert H. *The Breakthrough Strategy*. Cambridge, Massachusetts, 1988. A bit misleadingly titled, this book is about implementing major organizational change through a chain of small wins that builds confidence and ultimately creates organizational capability. This is an effective technique for a program, such as risk management, that often has to overcome cultural hurdles.

Smith, Preston G. and Reinertsen, Donald G. *Developing Products in Half the Time.* New York: John Wiley & Sons, 1998. See Chapter 15 of this book for details on the pilot project strategy and continuous improvement, as well as more supplementary readings on these subjects. Also see the forewords in this edition and the 1991 edition for more on the commitment required for successful implementation of such programs.

12
CASE STUDIES FROM ALLIED FIELDS

To further illustrate how the project risk management process and the Standard Risk Model described in this book can be applied, we provide two case studies. The first is a manufacturing risk of an inability to meet production volume targets. The second deals with the software risk of insufficient memory on a hardware module to support the required software features. Both of these case studies derive from actual projects.

Manufacturing Ramp-Up Case Study

Any product manufactured in large quantities creates a project environment that is rich with risk drivers. Even a cleanly executed product development cycle can be for naught if manufacturing and supply chain processes are not capable of meeting demand. Against this must be balanced the opposite risk of excess manufacturing capacity should the product not receive market acceptance.

SCOPE

In this case study, a consumer product is being prepared for commercialization. The manufacturing team is using a phased product development process and is just about to complete the planning phase of the project, five months prior to launching the product. We will follow the team's progress through the entire risk management process for one particular risk. In reality, the team will have identified several risks, but we will only focus on one. Therefore, we only mention the prioritization and risk mapping exercise for completeness.

STEP 1: IDENTIFY RISK

The manufacturing team has identified a risk that has the potential to dramatically affect its ability to deliver product. They have stated the risk event as: "Manufacturing capacity will only meet 45 percent of forecasted quantities for the first three months of production." Their impact statement is: "Gross margin will be €5,322,429 (euros), which is a 55 percent reduction from the business case target of €11,827,620." Notice that the total loss can be extracted from the impact statement already by subtracting the reduced gross margin from the business case target. Therefore, the team sets the total loss (L_t) to €6,505,191.

STEP 2: ANALYZE RISK

Next, the team must justify why they believe this risk has merit and must be managed actively. Accordingly, they generate risk event drivers, which are:

1. New manufacturing line installed, which is capable of producing 5,000 units per week.
2. Historically, there is a 70 percent chance that a new manufacturing line will operate at only 45 percent of rated capacity for the first three months of production.
3. Third-shift personnel have not been trained to operate new manufacturing equipment.
4. One custom parts vendor has not been evaluated to determine its capacity to meet our forecast.

The team collectively reviews these risk event drivers to determine the risk event probability. However, they quickly realize that Driver 4 represents a problem, because they are missing a key piece of data. To determine manufacturing capacity, they must take into account not only their own manufacturing line capacity but also the capacity of vendors, particularly those supplying custom components. The materials representative accepts an action item—to work with this vendor to develop a capacity analysis. However, until that action is complete, the team decides to use history as a primary determinant for the probability. Driver 2 indicates that 70 percent of the time, when new products are being introduced, the manufacturing capacity is only 45 percent of the required output for the first three months of production. The team decides the P_e will be set to 0.7 (70 percent).

Next, they develop a set of impact drivers:

1. Business case forecasts the following quantities for the first three months of production: 5,000, 7,500, and 12,000 units.
2. Average sales price is €995, and the estimated cost of goods sold (COGS) is €512.24.
3. Sales confirmed forecast quantities; customers are eager to receive product.

Now they must establish the probability of impact, which is the probability of suffering the total loss, L_t, if the risk event occurs. They reason that if the total loss, as provided in the impact statement, is a 55 percent reduction in the gross margin during the first three months, and if production runs at only 45 percent of forecast, then this reduced gross margin is a certainty. Therefore, P_i will be set to unity (100 percent).

Finally, they calculate the expected loss. Recall that you calculate expected loss by multiplying the risk event probability, impact probability, and the total loss together. The following is the team's completed analysis:

$$L_e = P_e \times P_i \times L_t$$
$$= 0.7 \times 1.0 \times €6,505,191$$
$$= €4,553,634$$

Figure 12-1 is a representation of the completed analysis.

STEP 3: PRIORITIZE AND MAP RISK

In an actual project, your team will be working with several risks that have emerged from the risk analysis workshops. Using the expected loss value, the team will then rank the risks and apply expert judgment regarding which ones to manage actively. As an aid, the team will map the risks onto a risk map (see Figure 3-3) that uses likelihood ($P_e \times P_i$) on the y-axis and total loss on the x-axis. Using a threshold line, the team will manage actively those risks above the threshold. They will also consider for active management any catastrophic risks that may be below the threshold line. For this case study, the manufacturing team has determined, by using prioritization and risk mapping, that they will manage this risk actively.

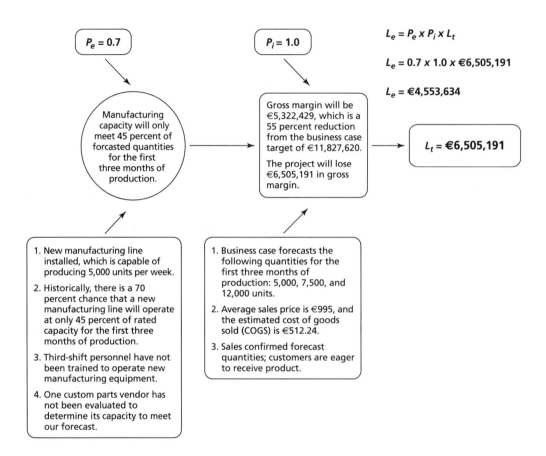

$$L_e = P_e \times P_i \times L_t$$

$$L_e = 0.7 \times 1.0 \times €6,505,191$$

$$L_e = €4,553,634$$

$P_e = 0.7$

$P_i = 1.0$

Manufacturing capacity will only meet 45 percent of forcasted quantities for the first three months of production.

Gross margin will be €5,322,429, which is a 55 percent reduction from the business case target of €11,827,620.

The project will lose €6,505,191 in gross margin.

$L_t = €6,505,191$

1. New manufacturing line installed, which is capable of producing 5,000 units per week.

2. Historically, there is a 70 percent chance that a new manufacturing line will operate at only 45 percent of rated capacity for the first three months of production.

3. Third-shift personnel have not been trained to operate new manufacturing equipment.

4. One custom parts vendor has not been evaluated to determine its capacity to meet our forecast.

1. Business case forecasts the following quantities for the first three months of production: 5,000, 7,500, and 12,000 units.

2. Average sales price is €995, and the estimated cost of goods sold (COGS) is €512.24.

3. Sales confirmed forecast quantities; customers are eager to receive product.

Figure 12-1. A manufacturing risk is decomposed into its constituent components so that it can be managed actively. If the risk event occurs, the manufacturing team could lose €6,505,191; however, the expected loss is €4,553,634.

STEP 4: PLAN RESOLUTION

The manufacturing team has selected the risks they will manage actively, and now they decide what to do about them. However, some decisions regarding resolution have already been made. For instance, they have implicitly made the decision to accept those risks not on the top 10 list. Also, remember the materials representative who had the action item to work with the custom part vender to determine their capacity to meet our forecast? That is an example of doing research to resolve a risk.

We follow our manufacturing risk, which is now on the top 10 list. Each risk event and impact driver is evaluated for any action that can be taken to modify it to decrease its associated probability. The first risk event driver deals with the capacity of the newly installed manufacturing line. The current capacity rating is 5,000 units per week, or 20,000 units per month, which is more than adequate to cover peak needs in the third month's forecast of 12,000. No action is needed for this driver. The next driver states that, with 70 percent probability, during the first three months of production, new lines historically run at about of 45 percent of capacity. Because this is historical information, no direct action can be taken on this driver, but the team must determine why this poor performance occurs.

The team digs into this and finds that two issues arise continually, causing low capacity on new lines: failure to adequately train people to operate the new manufacturing equipment and failure of custom parts vendors to ramp up sufficiently to meet forecast. Risk event Driver 3 shows that the third shift personnel have not been trained on the new equipment. This prompts the team to develop a risk action plan to schedule training for the third shift, which will change this risk event driver.

Now the team pursues the other issue they discovered, that custom parts vendors typically do not ramp up adequately. Data from the materials representative who has analyzed the vendor's capacity shows that the vendor can only produce about 85 percent of the needed quantity of parts for the first three months. Since the team is about six months from the launch, they have sufficient time to work with the vendor to increase its capacity. The team develops a risk action plan to share the forecast with the vendor, and in addition they decide to sign a letter of intent now to purchase the needed quantities. As a result, the vendor agrees to increase capacity to meet the forecasted quantities.

Even though the team has developed what appear to be effective risk action plans to prevent the risk event from occurring, the probability of the risk event did not drop to zero. Consequently, they pursue contingency plans in the event that production targets still cannot be met. Recall that contingency plans act on the impact drivers. The first impact driver deals with the forecasted quantities from the business case. One possible action is to verify the accuracy of the quantities; however, impact Driver 3 states that this step was already pursued. In addition, Sales has re-iterated customers' desire to get this product as soon as possible. Thus, the team sees no opportunity in Driver 1 and moves on.

The second impact driver states the average sales price and the cost of goods sold. From this driver, two possible contingency plans emerge. One is to raise the average sales price to maintain gross margin if sales volume drops. However, the success of this plan hinges on any forward pricing commitments with customers and the value proposition to be used. Another possible contingency plan is to find possible reductions in the cost of goods sold. A final alternative would be to do nothing and simply accept the lost margin. The team decides to form a "tiger team" to review any ways to reduce the cost of goods sold.

Figure 12-2 is the risk tracking spreadsheet that will be used to monitor the risk.

STEP 5: MONITOR RISK

The manufacturing team has developed a set of risk action plans for both prevention and contingency. They next implement those plans effectively to reduce the risk likelihood. On the prevention side, the team monitors training activities for operators on the new manufacturing line, and they determine that all operators have successfully completed the training and are certified to support operations of the new line. The second prevention plan—increasing the capacity of the custom parts vendor—turns out to be equally successful. The materials representative and the vendor develop a system to provide timely forecast data to ensure that all custom parts will be available when needed. Consequently, the custom parts vendor is fully prepared to support launch of the new product on schedule.

The team closes the risk after the first production run in September, which shows they have met the needed quantities. Even though risk technically still exists for the next two months of initial production, the team feels confident that the prevention plans put into place will successfully mitigate the likelihood of the risk occurring.

As part of the monitoring step, the team scans regularly for new risks or changes in existing risks. Frequently they ask themselves, "Is anything connected with this risk leading to new risks that we should consider?" If

Risk Identifier	Priority	Risk Owner
M5	1	Sally Russell

Risk Event: Manufacturing capacity will only meet 45 percent of forecasted quantities for the first three months of production.

Impact: Gross margin will be €5,322,429, which is a 55 percent reduction from the business case target of €11,827,620. The project will lose €6,505,191 in gross margin.

	Date Opened	Date Closed	Risk Status	Actual Loss	
	April 2	Sept. 3	Closed		0
Monitor Dates	P_e	P_i		Euros L_t	Euros L_e
April 2	0.7	1		€6,505,191	€4,553,634
May 7	0.9	1		€6,505,191	€5,854,672
June 4	0.9	1		€6,505,191	€5,854,672
July 2	0.5	1		€6,505,191	€3,252,596
Aug. 5	0.1	1		€5,877,697	€587,770
Sept. 3	0.1	1		€5,877,697	€587,770

Risk Event Drivers	Prevention Plans	Impact Drivers	Contingency Plans
1. New manufacturing line installed, which is capable of producing 5000 units per week.	1. No action needed.	1. Business case forecasts the following quantities for the first three months of production: 5000, 7500, and 1200 units.	1. No action needed.
2. Historically, there is a 70 percent chance that a new manufacturing line will operate at 45 percent of its rated capacity for the first three months of production.	2. Perform root-cause analysis on why past capacity levels were below required needs. Status—April 30: Team has determined the primary causes for reduced quantities have been the lack of training for operators and failure of custom parts vendors to ramp up sufficiently to meet forecast. This is consistent with our identified risk event drivers. We now believe the P_e has increased to 0.9.	2. Average sales price is €995, and the estimated cost of goods sold (COGS) is €512.24.	2. Form a "tiger team" to develop a set of cost reduction actions to reduce the COGS value. Status—August 1: We have identified three components that can be substituted for lower cost parts. By making these changes we can reduce COGS to €486.63. This will decrease the total loss by €627,494.
3. Third shift personnel have not been trained to operate new manufacturing equipment.	3. Develop a training plan for 3rd shift. Training is targeted from July 8 to July 12. We are planning a prototype build from July 15 to July 19; at this time we will certify operators for all shifts for the new manufacturing line. Status—July 22: We have completed the training and certified 19 operators to support the new manufacturing line. We believe P_e has been reduced to 0.1.	3. Sales confirmed forecast quantities; customers are eager to receive product.	3. No action needed.
4. One custom parts vendor has not been evaluated to determine its capacity to meet our forecast.	4. Conducted a capacity study which revealed only 85 percent capacity could be achieved. Status: July 2—The vendor will increase capacity if we share the forecast with them, and sign a letter of intent now to purchase the needed quantities.		

Figure 12-2. This is a completed example of a tracking spreadsheet for actively managing a manufacturing capacity risk.

we were looking at the whole project, we would find them doing the same for any other new risk in the project.

In summary, the manufacturing team was successful in preventing the risk from occurring. In addition, the team still went ahead and executed the contingency plan of forming the "tiger team" to evaluate ways to reduce the COGS. Their efforts resulted in the COGS being reduced from €512.24 to €486.63, which increased the gross margin for the first three months of production, by €627,494.

Embedded Software Development Case Study

SCOPE

In this case study, a software development team has been challenged to release a new product by reusing an existing hardware module loaded with a new software feature set. However, as software features increase in complexity, the amount of memory required to store the code usually increases as well. In this example, we follow a software development team and their hardware counterparts as they manage this risk. As before, this project is close to completing its planning phase.

The product is an embedded real-time system that comprises several digital signal processors and application-specific integrated circuits, along with a microprocessor and an array of flash memory. In addition, software applications residing on the module control system behavior, drive the user interface, and interface with an on-board database that is also stored in the flash memory.

STEP 1: IDENTIFY RISK

Software development has identified a risk that could stretch the software integration phase significantly (by 30 workdays). Their *risk event* is: "The current hardware module will not provide enough flash memory to support new software applications." Their *impact* statement is: "The software integration phase will need an additional 30 workdays because the hardware module needs to be modified for additional flash memory." In this case study, the total loss is readily apparent, so the team sets the total loss (L_t) to 30 workdays.

STEP 2: ANALYZE RISK

Next the team must justify why they believe this risk has merit and must be managed actively. They first develop the following risk event drivers:

1. Four large software features are being introduced.
2. Feasibility study indicates the four new software features and database will consume approximately 30 percent of current flash memory.
3. The existing feature set and database already consume 60 percent of current flash memory.
4. A new database is being introduced since the manufacturer is phasing out the current database system.

The team then collectively reviews the risk event drivers to determine the risk event probability. The first risk event driver is simply a statement of fact, which the team accepts as part of the project objectives. The second and third risk event drivers will increase the probability of the risk event. Since the feasibility study was completed prior to any new software being developed, the team estimated that when combined, the old and new feature set, along with the new database, should consume about 90 percent of the available flash memory. This will leave a 10 percent margin for any errors that may exist in the feasibility study (the software team prefers to keep a 20 percent error margin at this stage of the project). Based on group consensus, the team believes they are running a 0.9 (90 percent) chance (which is the value they assign to P_e) that the hardware module's flash memory will be insufficient to support their new software applications and the new database system.

They turn to their impact drivers, which are:

1. Hardware engineering is currently working on another high-priority project.
2. Hardware module redesign to add more memory will require 10 workdays of effort.
3. Printed circuit board (PCB) manufacturing will require 10 workdays to build new PCB.

4. Manufacturing will need 5 workdays to build the hardware module with new PCB.

5. Hardware test group will need to perform 5 workdays of unit testing before the new hardware module is handed off to the software development team.

The software development team then estimates the probability of the impact if the risk event occurs. In this particular case study, the efforts required to "spin" the board to add more flash memory are fairly well defined due to the known task durations. The team believes there is a 0.9 (90 percent) chance (which is the value they assign to P_i) that it will take 30 workdays to identify the changes, build the new module, unit test it, and return it to the software team so they can continue with their software integration efforts.

Finally, they calculate the expected loss:

$$L_e = P_e \times P_i \times L_t$$
$$= 0.9 \times 0.9 \times 30 \text{ workdays}$$
$$= 24.3 \text{ workdays}$$

Figure 12-3 is a representation of the completed analysis.

STEP 3: PRIORITIZE AND MAP RISK

In an actual project, your team will be working with several risks that have emerged from the risk analysis workshops. Using the expected loss value, the team will then rank the risks and apply expert judgment regarding which risks to manage actively. As an aid, the team will map the risks onto a risk map (see Figure 3-3) that uses likelihood ($P_e \times P_i$) on the y-axis and total loss on the x-axis. Using a threshold line, the team will actively manage those risks above the threshold. They will also consider for active management any catastrophic risks that may be below the threshold line.

For this case study, prioritization and risk mapping have determined that the software development team will manage this risk actively.

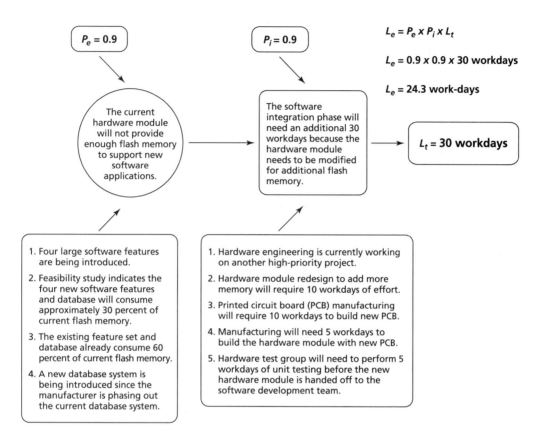

Figure 12-3. A software risk is decomposed into its constituent components so it may be managed actively. If the risk event occurs, the software development team could lose 30 workdays due to the software integration schedule slipping; however, the expected loss is 24.3 workdays.

STEP 4: PLAN RESOLUTION

First, the team takes action on the risk events by developing prevention plans. Their second step is to develop contingency plans if the risk event still occurs despite the prevention plans. In reviewing the feature set, the team questions the need for one of the features, so a plan is put into place with the marketing team to verify the feature set with a select few customers; however, the customer response is overwhelming—all four features are needed.

The next driver is a result of the feasibility study indicating that 30 percent of the current flash memory is needed to support the new features and database. Since all the new features are needed, this driver is considered by the software development team to be a constraint of the current platform, so no action is taken.

Driver 3 shows that 60 percent of the current flash memory is already being consumed with the existing feature set and database. However, the team develops a prevention plan to review all the source code to determine if any code is unused or will not be needed in this new product. If they find a significant amount of "dead code," they could remove it to make more space available for the new software and database.

The last risk event driver deals with the introduction of a new database to replace the current one, due to obsolescence. The team decides to explore if any new data compression or data structures may be incorporated in the new database software, allowing a more space-efficient database design and thus reducing the burden on the flash memory.

Next—despite their efforts to prevent the risk event from occurring—the team moves to develop contingency plans. They review the impact drivers, which deal with project assignment for hardware engineering and durations to "spin" the printed circuit board. Since these drivers reside with the hardware engineering team, the software team engages them to explore alternatives to reduce the intervals. From this effort emerge two contingency plans:

1. Expedite the building of the printed circuit board and the hardware module itself.
2. Start the software integration with the current modules but do not load all the software onto the hardware module until the new boards arrive.

The team decides against the first plan, since history has shown that when printed circuited boards and hardware modules are expedited, manufacturing quality decreases significantly, which ultimately causes more rework. The team decides to proceed with the second contingency plan. If the hardware module lacks sufficient memory, software integration will continue with smaller software loads until the new hardware module is ready. By adjusting the load-building schedule and then introducing the new hardware module near the middle of the software integration phase, they could reduce the schedule slip to 15 workdays. Even though the entire 30 workday slip was not absorbed, the team should be able to mitigate half of the original total loss. However, recall that the first impact driver shows that hardware engineering is engaged in another high-priority project, so the software and hardware teams believe they have a 50 percent chance of being able to reduce the total loss to 15 workdays, due to competing hardware resources. Accordingly, P_i is set to 0.5 and L_t is set to 15 workdays.

Figure 12-4 is the risk tracking spreadsheet that will be used to monitor the risk.

STEP 5: MONITOR RISK

The software development team has developed a set of risk action plans for both prevention and contingency. The primary metric they will monitor is flash memory usage. The team puts a process in place to build software loads frequently and monitor how much memory remains as the software size increases. The team defines a trigger point to enact the contingency plan if they detect that running out of flash memory is inevitable.

As the project progressed, the team's prevention plans paid off: when they reviewed the existing source code, they found that 30 percent of the software was dead code not needed in the new product. They removed the dead code, which freed up a significant amount of flash memory and allowed the software team to stay within their 20 percent margin. Next, the team did find a new data compression function in the new database system that could be used on a part of the database having less stringent requirements in the real-time domain.

The team's monitoring step also included ongoing alertness for other factors that might change this risk, such as new software features that might be proposed. Had they identified new risks, they would have been entered into the system.

In summary, the software development team successfully prevented the risk from occurring. The team decided that as part of the next release,

Risk Identifier	Priority	Risk Owner	Date Opened	Date Closed	Risk Status	Actual Loss	
						Workdays L_t	Workdays L_e
SW1	3	Victor Moran	Oct. 10	Sept. 28	Closed		0

Risk Event: The current hardware module will not provide enough flash memory to support new software applications.

Impact: The software integration phase will need an additional 30 workdays because the hardware module needs to be modified for additional flash memory.

Monitor Dates	P_e	P_i	L_t Workdays	L_e Workdays
Aug. 10	0.9	0.9	30	24.30
Aug. 24	0.9	0.9	30	24.30
Sept. 7	0.7	0.9	30	18.90
Sept. 14	0.1	0.9	30	2.70
Sept. 28	0.1	0.5	15	0.75

Risk Event Drivers

1. Four large software features are being introduced.

2. Feasibility study indicates the four new software features and database will consume approximately 30 percent of current flash memory.

3. The existing feature set and database already consume 60 percent of current flash memory.

4. A new database system is being introduced since the manufacturer is phasing out the current database system.

Prevention Plans

1. Determine if any of the features can be dropped from the product scope.
Status—August 24: Marketing and engineering met with customers to review the problems the defined feature set is targeted to solve. Several options were proposed but the currently defined features are definitely needed. All features must be supported.

2. No action taken. This is a constraint of the project.

3. Form a team (software, product management, and marketing will compose the team) to review the entire source code to determine if any of the current features can be dropped to free up memory space. This action needs to be completed by Sept. 14.
Status—Sept. 12: The team has identified nine features that will not be needed in the defined solution space for the customers. This will free up 30 percent of the flash memory. The team believes this will drop P_e by about 50 percent.

4. Investigate if the database system provides any new data compression algorithms or data structures that are more memory efficient. Engineering will need to complete this task by Sept. 7.
Status—Sept. 5: No new data structures are being introduced; however, a new data compression algorithm exists. We are going to target the event logging portion of the database, which does not have real-time access requirements. We believe this will reduce P_e by 20 percent.

Impact Drivers

1. Hardware engineering is currently working on another high-priority project.

2. Hardware module redesign to add more memory will require 10 workdays of effort.

3. Printed circuit board (PCB) manufacturing will require 10 workdays to build new PCB.

4. Manufacturing will need five workdays to build the hardware module with new PCB.

5. Hardware test group will need to perform five workdays of unit testing before the new hardware module is handed off to the software development team.

Contingency Plans

1. No action taken. Hardware resources are currently on the critical path for the other high-priority project. They may become available in the middle of Sept.

2. No action taken. We believe this is an accurate estimate of the work.

3. Review if we can expedite the building of the PCB with our subcontractor.
Status—Aug. 17: Past data indicates that quality problems have been introduced when we expedite PCBs, causing us to perform rework and sometimes even the need to build additional PCBs. The team has decided not to pursue this action plan.

4. No action taken. We believe this is an accurate estimate of the work.

5. Software development team will rework the load build strategy to focus on building smaller loads that should fit within the current memory constraints. A schedule will be developed showing the new hardware being introduced in the middle of software integration.
Status—Sept. 25: The new schedule shows we could mitigate the slip by 15 workdays. The team is reducing P_i to 50 percent and L_t to 15 workdays.

Figure 12-4. This is a completed example of a tracking spreadsheet for actively managing a flash memory limitation risk.

they would go ahead and add more memory. Interestingly, that decision—intended to preclude a risk in the future—created a new risk for them, because the installed base may not be able to use any software that requires expanded flash memory. But that is another story.

Summary

In this chapter, we applied the risk management process described in this book to demonstrate how the technique can be applied to very different projects. The case studies presented here are adapted from actual risks that were successfully prevented. In both of these examples, we illustrated how being proactive during the planning phase of the project can enhance sales, save significant time, and greatly minimize the firefighting so characteristic of most projects as they are about to be released.

Supplementary Reading

(For additional information on managing software project risks, see "Supplementary Reading" for Chapters 1, 4, and 8.)

Ashley, Steven. Concorde's comeback. *Scientific American* 285(2):12–13 (August 2001). On July 25, 2000, a Concorde supersonic transport crashed in Paris due to a tire failure and resulting debris that ultimately brought the plane down. We suggest that you use the details in this article as an exercise to identify the drivers. Then formulate prevention plans (prevent tire failure) and contingency plans (avert a crash if the tire fails).

Jones, Richard B. *Risk-Based Management: A Reliability-Centered Approach.* Houston, Texas: Gulf Publishing, 1995. A well-written book focused on manufacturing reliability and maintainability risks. Jones provides a five-step process, but it is not the core of his book and is rather different than the process we suggest for managing a project.

Regnier, Pat. Will Concorde fly? *Time* (Atlantic Edition) 158(5):32–33 (July 30, 2001). Provides additional details on the Concorde crash and fixes.

GLOSSARY

Action plan: A resolution strategy to reduce risk likelihood or consequences.

Actual loss: The magnitude of the realized loss value accrued when a risk event and impact actually occurs (compare with *Total loss*).

Checklist: A list of important items that should be adhered to, such as a pilot's checklist. See *Prompt list*.

Contingency plan: An action plan that is enacted after the risk event has occurred; it is usually designed to address impact drivers.

Critical path: A sequence of activities in a project such that if any activity in the sequence slips, the completion date of the project will slip by the same amount.

Driver: Either a risk event driver or an impact driver.

Expected loss: An overall measure of the average loss associated with a risk, taking into account the probability of risk event and the probability of impact.

Impact (of a risk): The consequence or potential loss that might result if a risk event occurs.

Impact driver: Something existing in the project environment that leads one to believe that a particular impact could occur.

Issue: An item like a risk, except that it is certain to occur.

Iteration: Making an initial assumption, verifying it, revising it as needed, until the assumption holds reasonably well. Necessary for innovation.

Management by walking around (MBWA): Management receiving first-hand, unfiltered information on progress and risk by visiting developers informally.

Prevention plan: An action plan aimed at reducing the probability that the risk event will occur or reducing its impact if it does occur; it is usually designed to address risk event drivers.

Probability of impact: The likelihood that an impact will occur, given that its risk event occurs.

Probability of risk event: The likelihood that a risk event will occur.

Prompt list: A list created by the present organization to remind it of similar historical issues that should perhaps be under consideration currently, such as a list of recent supplier difficulties. See *Checklist*.

Reserve: A kitty of money, time (a schedule buffer), or other loss quantity provided to cover risks you accept and risks not fully mitigated, along with some protection against unknown risks that may occur.

Risk: The possibility that an undesired outcome—or the absence of a desired outcome—disrupts your project. A risk always reflects uncertainty, a potential loss, and a time component.

Risk avoidance: An action plan that avoids a risk by reversing decisions that caused the risk to arise in the first place.

Risk event: The happening or state that triggers the loss.

Risk event driver: Something existing in the project environment that leads one to believe that a particular risk event could occur.

Risk identifier: A unique tag, such as R1, R2, or R3, attached to each risk when it is identified and carried through the process to identify this risk as others are added and removed.

Risk likelihood: The combination of: 1) the probability of risk event and 2) the probability of impact multiplied together.

Risk management: The activity of identifying and controlling undesired project outcomes proactively.

Risk management plan: A subset of a project plan that defines the strategy for how risks are to be managed.

Risk mitigation: Action plans that mitigate a risk by developing prevention and contingency plans along with adequate reserves of time and money for unknown risks.

Risk reduction leverage: Ratio of the benefit derived from an action plan relative to the cost of implementing or executing it. The benefit may be only partial.

Risk redundancy: An action plan that provides redundant paths to increase the likelihood of success in resolving a risk.

Risk transfer: An action plan that transfers a risk to another entity.

Sticky: A slip of paper with a strip of removable adhesive on the back, such as a Post-It® note.

Top 10 list: A list of a project's risks that are being actively managed. The list actually may have more or less than 10 risks on it, and the number of risks on it normally will decrease as the project reaches completion.

Total loss: The magnitude of the actual loss value accrued when a risk event occurs, measured in days or money (other quantities could used, but we recommend consistently using one unit—for instance, workdays *or* euros—throughout a project so you can compare risks easily).

Trigger: A time, milestone, or condition that initiates a mitigation plan.

Index

Books from Productivity Press

Productivity Press publishes books that empower individuals and companies to achieve excellence in quality, productivity, and the creative involvement of all employees. Through steadfast efforts to support the vision and strategy of continuous improvement, Productivity Press delivers today's leading-edge tools and techniques gathered directly from industry leaders around the world.

To request a complete catalog of our publications call us toll free at **800-394-6868** or visit us online at **www.productivityinc.com**

Cost Half –The Method for Radical Cost Reduction
Toshio Suzue

Cost Half is an innovative tool designed for actualizing the lean production system. It furnishes the manufacturer with a set of cost reduction methods designed to achieve unprecedented levels of systematic organization and operational profitability. The Cost Half approach is a radical, "greedy" approach that focuses on developing three interrelated strengths to ensure stable business results. That is, Cost Half puts you on the road to increasing market development strength, improving competitive quality, and maintaining competitive cost.
ISBN 1-56327-249-0 | 2002 | Stock # COSTHA - $45.00

Value Stream Management – Eight Steps to Planning, Mapping, and Sustaining Lean Improvements
Don Tapping, Tom Luyster, and Tom Shuker
Value Stream Management is a complete system that provides a clear path to lean implementation, ensuring quick deployment and great benefits. *Value Stream Management* shows you how to use mapping as part of a **complete system** for lean implementation. The central feature of this illustrative and engaging book is the **value stream management storyboard**, a tool representing an eight-step process for lean implementation. The storyboard brings together people, tools, metrics, and reporting into one visual document.
ISBN 1-56327-245-8 | 2002 | Stock # VALUE - $ 45.00

Make No Mistake! An Outcome-Based Approach to Mistake-Proofing
C. Martin Hinckley

Do you spend a great deal of time reworking products in the manufacturing process? Do defective products reach your customers? If the answer to either of those questions is yes, then much of the productive capacity of your manufacturing process is going to waste. Imagine the potential that would be unleashed if every product that rolled out of your plant came out right the first time – without rework, without defects. Author C. Martin Hinckley has gathered here – for the first time in a single source – the best methods for reducing complexity, variation, confusion, and the other root causes of defects.
ISBN 1-56327-227-X | 2001 | Stock # MISTAKE - $75.00

Reorganizing the Factory: Competing Through Cellular Manufacturing
Nancy Hyer and Urban Wemmerlöv

Cellular manufacturing principles, applied to either administrative work or production, are fundamental building blocks for lean and quick response organizations. Reorganizing the Factory is the definitive reference book in this important area. *Reorganizing the Factory's* detailed and comprehensive "life cycle" approach will take readers from basic concepts and advantages of cells through the process of justifying, designing, implementing, operating, and improving this new type of work organization in each unique environment.
ISBN 1-56327-228-8 | 2001 | Stock # REORG $ 90.00

DOE Simplified – Practical Tools for Effective Experimentation
Mark J. Anderson and Patrick J. Whitcomb

Design of Experiment (DOE) is a planned approach for determining cause and effect relationships. The tool can be applied to any process with measurable input and outputs. DOE Simplified is a comprehensive new introductory text that is geared for readers with minimal statistical backgrounds. Filled with fun anecdotes and sidebars, the text cuts through the complexities of this powerful improvement tool.
ISBN 1-56327-225-3 | 2000 | Stock # DOESI - $39.95

Toyota Production System – Beyond Large-Scale Production
Taiichi Ohno

Taiichi Ohno is considered the inventor of the Toyota Production
System (known as Just-In-Time manufacturing) and lean manufacturing.
In *Toyota Production System,* the creator of just-in-time production for
Toyota reveals the origins, daring innovations and ceaseless evolution of
the Toyota system into a full management system.
ISBN 0-915299-14-3 | 1988 | Stock #: OTPS - $ 45.00

Becoming Lean – Inside Stories of U.S. Manufacturers
Jeffrey Liker

This best-seller contains performance records and real numbers to back
up the power of going lean, lessons learned in the process of change
(both logistics and people issues), and a realistic account of the journey
to lean. This is the first book to provide technical descriptions of successful solutions and performance improvements. It's also the first book
to go beyond snapshots and includes powerful first-hand accounts of
the complete process of change; its impact on the entire organization;
and the rewards and benefits of becoming lean.
ISBN 1-56327-173-7 | Stock # LEAN - $ 35.00